DATE DUE

RING IN
THE
JUBILEE

RING IN THE JUBILEE

The Epic of America's Liberty Bell

CHARLES MICHAEL BOLAND

THE CHATHAM PRESS, INC.
RIVERSIDE, CONNECTICUT

SBN 85699-054-X (cloth edition)
SBN 85699-055-8 (paper edition)

Library of Congress Catalog Card Number: 72-80407

Printed in the United States of America

ACKNOWLEDGEMENTS

Tracking the story of the Liberty Bell has been an exciting and remarkably enlightening undertaking, and a great many people have contributed to the substance of this volume. First of all, a special vote of thanks is due Lucien Agniel for providing much of the early research and my editor, John V. Hinshaw, who searched for Pass and Stow. Deep appreciation goes to the staff members of Independence Hall National Historical Park, especially Martin I. Yoelson, Gregorio S. A. Carrera and Penelope H. Batcheler, for their assistance and personal interest in the project; to the staff of the Historical Society of Pennsylvania, especially Peter Parker, John H. Platt, Jr., and Anthony Roth, for providing original documents and aiding in the research; to Douglas Hughes, Master Founder at Whitechapel Bell Foundry, London, for his valuable contributions on early and modern bell casting; to Joan St. George Saunders for her meticulous research in the British Museum and elsewhere; and to Richard J. Guilfoyle for his critique of the manuscript.

CHARLES MICHAEL BOLAND
March, 1973

Contents

Preface

I N 1776 THE FINEST STATESMEN THE COLONIES COULD MUSTER
gathered in Philadelphia to protest the demands of the British
Crown and concluded by declaring the American Colonies to
be "free and independent states." Had these men attempted to create
a symbol for the freedoms they boldly espoused, it is doubtful they
would have chosen the Bell which hung above them in the State
House steeple. To them it was just another bell; a good one, to be
sure, but they considered it no more than an instrument to announce
news or call meetings — if, in truth, they gave it any thought at all.

Today this same Bell stands in quiet splendor, a national treasure
sheltered and guarded beneath the tower of Independence Hall. The
entire building has been turned back in time to 1776, skillfully re-
modeled to its last molding and fixture. In contrast to the newness
of the paint on the walls around it, the Bell looks shabby. It is nicked,
scratched and gouged; a jagged crack reaches from the brim to the
inscription; and the only sound it has emitted for over 125 years has
been in response to muted tappings with a special hammer. But the
old State House Bell is now the Liberty Bell, the most widely known,
revered, duplicated and misunderstood bell in the world.

The Bell has had a remarkable history. Its birth twice miscarried; it has been marked for destruction by its enemies in early and modern times, and nearly sold for scrap by unimpressed friends. It has spawned myriad legends concerning its many ringings, the historic dramas it witnessed, its final cracking and the very name by which it is now known.

Perhaps the secret behind this famous Bell lies in the nature of the "liberties" for which it stands and which its motto, "Proclaim Liberty throughout all the Land," has represented. For throughout the history of the Bell there have been three basic liberties embraced: the religious liberty of William Penn's colony; the political liberty of young America; and the liberty of Blacks from slavery. In total, these liberties include men and women of all creeds, all parties and all races. Their dreams and aspirations may differ, but the underlying freedom which makes them possible is forged into this one Bell, a symbol not only for Americans but for all the peoples of the world.

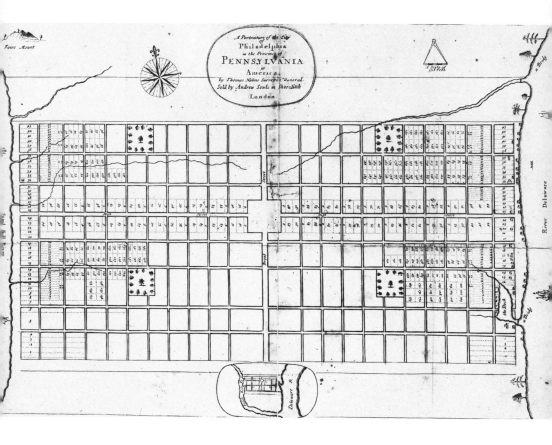

Thomas Holme's 1683 plan for Penn's "Greene Country Towne." In his book *Design of Cities,* architect Edmund N. Bacon speculates that this plan, as well as that of Savannah, Georgia, was strongly influenced by designs for Roman cities created by Marcus Vitruvius in the first century, B.C. A book of Vitruvius' city plans, *L'Architettura* by Pietro Cataneo, was first published in Venice in 1567. Whether Holme had direct knowledge of this book when he laid out Philadelphia is unknown, but the basic elements of Philadelphia's geometrical city blocks and parks are present in *L'Architettura* and thus the modular rhythm of Roman design may have found expression in the New World at an early date. *National Park Service.*

Seed
of a
Nation

I N THE YEAR 1751, THE LEGISLATORS OF THE PROVINCE OF
   Pennsylvania found themselves occupied with the problem of
   obtaining a suitable bell for their new State House on Chestnut
Street, between Fifth and Sixth streets in the city of Philadelphia.

There already was a bell in the yard of the State House which, it
is believed, had been brought from England by William Penn and
hung from the branch of a tree. While this bell was adequate for a
small village, its peal could not be heard at great distances; furthermore, its size and tone lacked the dignity appropriate to a State
House bell. The legislators therefore authorized the building of a
bell tower adjoining their meeting place and sought to find a new
bell whose sound would be audible throughout the rapidly expanding city.

In Colonial times, bells were the prime means of communication,
and they had served this purpose for centuries before. It was not until
the invention of the telegraph, and later radio and television, that
news could be disseminated quickly. All of the newspapers were
weeklies and, because of the time lag between receiving the news,

printing it and then distributing the sheets, they could not be considered a fast means of reaching the public. Every community, including the largest city, depended upon the sound of bells to call its council or assembly into session, to announce events of immediate importance such as an attack by hostile forces, to toll the death of a prominent citizen and, of course, to call the population to worship.

The pealing of the assembly bell gathered citizens from far and near to hear news on the spot. They, in turn, spread the word to others. The method of ringing to differentiate the nature of events varied from community to community, but some rings were unmistakable; a muffled toll invariably indicated a solemn or mournful happening while a series of quick rings and pauses spelled out in code the occurrence of a fire and its location. The State House Bell eventually had another code peculiar to itself: it was rung at intervals of three and five minutes, alternately, to call people to the polls on election days. Town-hall bells also were used to strike three daytime signals: six in the morning to arouse the people, noon, and nine P.M. curfew. Executions were announced by a toll of "three times three" for a man and "three times two" for a woman.

Announcement bells ranged all the way from the handbell of the town crier or night watch up to the massive, booming heralds in church steeples. In Philadelphia, most able-bodied males took turns at walking the night watch and ringing the bell to call time and weather and to warn of emergencies. By 1704, the city had grown so that ten night watchmen were needed — all volunteers. It was not until 1758 that the first paid night watchmen appeared.

But in 1751 the Pennsylvania legislators needed a new, distance-conquering bell for their expanding city. Unknowingly, through the words ordered inscribed on this Bell by their Speaker, Isaac Norris, they were to herald the coming independence of the American Colonies. A member of the Society of Friends and one of the leading citizens of the young colony, Norris' inscription was actually to be the second foretelling of independence; the first was manifest in the governmental ground rules laid down by Quaker William Penn, Proprietor of the Province of Pennsylvania and founder of Philadelphia, the City of Brotherly Love.

Almost all of the land now known as the Commonwealth of Pennsylvania was granted to William Penn in the year 1681 by King Charles II of England as payment for a sixteen-thousand-pound debt to Penn's father, Admiral Sir William Penn. Prior to that time, the land along the Delaware River had seen a stormy period of settlement which began in 1638 with the arrival of a party of Swedes under Peter Minuit. They built a fort at what is now Wilmington, Delaware, and began a lively trade with the Indians. This prosperity irritated the Dutch in Nieuw Amsterdam, who proceeded to build their own fort at the junction of the Delaware and Schuylkill rivers. Then the Swedes built a second fort; the Dutch followed suit and the feud was on. The Dutch were in control of the region when, in 1664, the British settled the matter by defeating them in Europe and gaining sovereignty over all Dutch territory in America, including both the Delaware River area and Nieuw Amsterdam, which became New York.

When the thirty-seven-year-old Penn, a tall, good-looking man dressed in the height of fashion, stood before the Privy Council in London to receive his grant, he proposed that the land be called "New Wales." The Welsh Secretary of the Council objected strongly to this proposal, for reasons unknown, and Penn then suggested that it be called "Sylvania," a Latin noun meaning woods or forest. The Council accepted the suggestion, but not without prefixing the name "Penn" to it, according to the King's desire to honor the Admiral. The use of his own name embarrassed the new proprietor; he did not want people to think him vain. He tried to coax the under-secretaries to reconsider their decision and ultimately offered them twenty guineas to change their minds. The bribe was disdained and the name became official — the only territory in the New World to bear the full name of its founder.

In a letter to Robert Turner, dated March 1, 1681, Penn described his battle with the Privy Council, but ended it on a bright — and prophetic — note:

> . . . [the grant] 'tis a clear and just thing, and my God that has given it me through many difficulties, will, I believe, bless and make it the seed of a nation. I shall have a tender care to the government, that it will be well laid at first.

William Penn (1644-1718) from a painting by Henry Inman, circa 1832.
National Park Service.

Penn's first act as proprietor was to send his cousin, William Markham, to the province as deputy governor. Markham arrived in July, 1681, took his oath of office and summoned a council of two Swedes and seven Englishmen. They selected Upland, later renamed Chester, as the first capital of the territory. The following spring, however, Penn decided to locate a new site for a "Great Towne" and sent three commissioners, William Crispin, John Bezar and Nathaniel Allen, who chose a strip of land between the Schuylkill River and the west bank of the Delaware as the most suitable location.

In June of that same year, 1682, Penn dispatched Thomas Holme to lay out the proposed city and on August 31 he himself sailed for America. Penn landed first at New Castle, proceeded to Upland and then to the site of his new capital, where he found the dedicated Holme busy laying out streets and settlers already building houses.

Being a fair and just man (belying the criticisms that were sometimes levelled at him because of his "foppish" dress), Penn quickly arranged a meeting with chiefs of the Lenni-Lenape, Susquehannock and Shawnee Indian tribes in order to purchase rights to their lands and to establish a treaty that would insure peace between their peoples for all time. The French statesman Voltaire described this compact as ". . . the only treaty never sworn to, and never broken."

In April, 1682, Penn drafted the province's first constitution, or *Frame of Government,* as it was called. In it, he wrote:

> . . . I know what is said by the several admirers of monarchy, aristocracy and democracy, which are the rule of one, a few, and many, and are the three common ideas of government, when men discuss that subject. But I choose to solve the controversy with this small distinction, and it belongs to all three: any government is free to the people under it (whatever be the frame) where the laws rule, and the people are a party to those laws, and more than this is tyranny, oligarchy and confusion.

Religious freedom was, of course, an important part of Penn's *Frame of Government.* Since he had published accounts of his territory before leaving England, its freedoms became widely known; they held a strong appeal as the word spread, and waves of immigrants poured into the colony — twenty-three vessels reached Philadelphia before December, 1682. By 1685, the province had more than seven thousand inhabitants, half of them British. Philadelphia itself burgeoned with three hundred houses and a population of about twenty-five hundred, including large numbers of Germans, Welsh, Scotch-Irish and French.

The new settlers were more than satisfied with what they found. Wild game of all kinds was abundant; wild pigeons, it was said, were so numerous that they were like clouds and wild turkeys were "so immoderately large and fat as to have weighed 46 pounds." Some, weighing thirty pounds, sold for two shillings, deer went for two shillings and a bushel of corn for two shillings and sixpence. One Mahlon Stacey, writing to an English friend, informed him that ". . . we have peaches by cartloads. The Indians bring us 7 or 8 fat bucks a day. Without rod or net we catch abundance of herrings . . . geese and ducks are plenty."

The site of the city itself was dramatically beautiful. The west bank of the Delaware rose sharply from the water and where it levelled off stood a magnificent forest of pine, whose fragrance filled the air and mingled with those of myriad wildflowers. The grass was green and lush, the water sweet. The "Greene Country Towne" that Penn had envisioned could hardly have been placed in a more appropriate setting.

Ironically, while the setting for Penn's new town was almost ideal, many early settlers were forced to live in caves gouged out of the sloping west bank of the river as they waited for houses to be built. The caves persisted for many years and, although some were filled in as their occupants moved to their new homes, others were inhabited by successive transients until the early eighteenth century. Problems arose when opportunists used them for dispensing spirits. Eventually, however, all the squatters were routed and the caves vanished as wharves and docks were built.

Penn had founded a colony that was to see many long years of peace and prosperity. His beliefs are summed up in one brief statement in a letter written to a Philadelphia judge around 1704:

I went thither to lay the foundation of a free colony for all mankind.

While his followers enjoyed the good life in the New World, Penn himself was destined to share only a small portion of it. From the day he sailed to Pennsylvania aboard the *Welcome,* the ship was blown by an evil wind; smallpox broke out and, of the one hundred immigrants Penn brought with him, thirty died en route.

His first stay in the new province lasted only three years, but during that time Penn organized his government along the lines he had first conceived, divided his lands into three counties (Philadelphia, Bucks and Chester) and issued writs for elections in those counties, as well as in the three Delaware counties. His *Frame of Government* called for a deputy governor, to be appointed by the proprietor, and for the election by the people of a provincial council and general assembly. The council would consist of seventy-two members; the assembly was not to exceed two hundred. A year after drafting his *Frame,* he revised it, reducing the council to eighteen and the assembly to thirty-six, with provisions for expansion to the original number based on population increase.

Returning to England in 1684, Penn busied himself with personal and business matters for a few years but, after the English Revolution of 1689, he was arrested several times, being suspected of treason and accused of too close a friendship with the ousted James II. In October, 1692, William and Mary took away his proprietorship of Pennsylvania and turned it over to the governor of New York, William Fletcher. In 1694, his rights were restored on the promise that he would remain loyal to the Crown and supervise his colony more carefully.

He returned to Pennsylvania in 1699 and again plunged into its government. On October 28, 1701, he drew up the *Charter of Privileges*. It was confirmed by the assembly and substantially remained the fundamental law of Pennsylvania until 1776.

The new *Charter* limited the powers of the governor and called for an annually-elected legislature of three members from each of the three counties. Religious freedom was guaranteed to all "who shall profess and acknowledge one Almighty God," but only Christians could hold office. This effectively shut out atheists from governing positions and, conceivably, any unreconstructed Indian who might seek a government post.

Penn's second visit to Pennsylvania was even shorter than the first. As soon as the new constitution was adopted in 1701, he sailed again for England where he faced monumental financial problems. Betrayed by an agent named Ford, Penn had become bankrupt and the astonishing Ford, who had mismanaged and stolen his money, had him seized while at a meeting — and thrown into debtors' prison. He was released after mortgaging his province for six thousand pounds. In 1712, he made the decision to sell his proprietary rights to Queen Anne, but suffered an apoplectic stroke which ended the negotiations and eventually led to his death in 1718. His second wife Hannah and his three sons succeeded to the proprietorship. On the deaths of Hannah and sons John and Richard, Richard's son John became proprietor jointly with the third son, Thomas.

In spite of the disasters that befell William Penn, the peace and prosperity he so desired for his colony continued through the family proprietorship of his wife, three sons and grandson. The French and Indian War raged in the western and northern parts of the province, but Philadelphia remained a placid little island, untouched except for reports of violence from nearby Bethlehem. Philadelphia was waiting for its patriots, its statesmen — and its Bell.

Get Us
a
Good Bell

D URING PENNSYLVANIA'S EARLY YEARS, ITS ASSEMBLY MET
casually in the homes of private citizens. Life was unhurried
in Philadelphia, and meetings at random places seemed per-
fectly in keeping with the times and the temperaments of the members. Occasionally, in a rare departure, the governing body met in
City Hall at Second and Market streets, perhaps to make their debate
more "official." But rumblings of dissatisfaction amid this apparent
serenity began to appear and, on October 16, 1728, the Assembly
surprised the citizens of Penn's town by passing a resolution requesting
the Governor and Council to consider moving the Assembly from
Philadelphia because of "indecencies" directed at the legislators by
"rude and disorderly persons." The nature of these indecencies was
never made clear but the aroused citizenry indicated that the Assembly should have its own building for meeting purposes.

Two valid reasons for erecting a permanent building for the Assembly were evident. First, the body would be protected against the
undescribed rowdyism and, second, a State House would certainly
lend dignity to the Assembly and imply unquestionable authority.

ABOVE: Isaac Norris, circa 1754. BELOW: The original design for the State House as submitted by Andrew Hamilton in 1732. Both *Historical Society of Pennsylvania.*

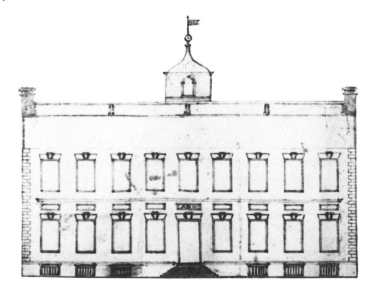

In addition, it would most surely keep the provincial capital in Philadelphia. Accordingly, the sum of two thousand pounds was appropriated for the building of such a meeting place. Strong disagreements quickly arose over the plans for the proposed edifice, but eventually differences were ironed out and the recommendations of Andrew Hamilton and his committee members, Dr. John Kearsley and Thomas Lawrence, were accepted. Edmund Woolley was designated as Master Carpenter with authority to employ several other carpenters, bricklayers and plasterers, and to procure the necessary materials.

It was 1736 before the province's governing body could meet in the new building, and even then the structure was by no means complete. Among the items of business at the first session was the appointment of Benjamin Franklin as clerk to the House of Representatives for the current year.

By 1751, as noted earlier, the legislators debated the idea of obtaining a bell for the State House, said bell to be put in a tower connected to the south side of the State House which would contain "a staircase, with a suitable place thereon for hanging a bell." The tower, ordered in 1749, was finished in 1752 and the small bell cupola originally atop the State House had been removed. A clock was ordered from a Philadelphia maker which, wrote Norris, "we expect will prove better than any they would send us from England. . . ."

It probably did not occur to the legislators to have a bell cast in the Colonies. While there were several bell foundries in New England, none had been established near Philadelphia. Blacksmiths abounded, but they could not handle such a complex task, and furthermore, all of the many bells then in the city had been cast in England. So the State House Trustees, acting under orders of the Assembly, prepared to contact the Assistant Colonial Agent in London so that he might order a bell from a British foundry.

Before the Revolution, each of the Colonies was represented in England by a Colonial Agent who acted on its behalf in obtaining materials needed in America, protesting impending legislation by the Crown that might be harmful to the colonists, or attending to whatever other business the Colony had in England. In 1751 Richard

Respect'd Aff'd Rob't Charles   Philad° nov'. 1 st. 1751

The Assembly having ordered us (the Superintendants of our Statehouse) to procure a Bell from England to be purchased for their use we take the Liberty to apply ourselves to thee to get us a good Bell of about two thousand pounds weight the cost of which we presume may amount to ab.t One hundred pounds sterl. or perhaps with the the Charges Something more and Accordingly we have now inclosed a first Bell of Exch.a giz.t John Perrin and Son on Mess.rs Thomas Flowerdew & Comp.a for £100— Sterling We would have chosen to remit a Larger Bill at this time, but will take care to furnish more as soon as we can be informed how much may be wanted

We hope and rely on thy care and assistance in this affair and that thou wilt procure and forward it by the first good Opp.o as our Workmen inform us it will be much less trouble to hang the Bell before their Scaffolds are struck from the Building where we intend to place it which will not be done 'till the end of next Summer or beginning of the Fall. Let the Bell be cast by the best Workmen & examined carefully before it is Shipped with the following words well shaped in large letters round it viz.t
BY order of the Assembly of the Province of Pensylvania for the State house in the City of Philad.° 1752
and Underneath,
Proclaim Liberty thro' all the Land to all the Inhabitants thereof Levit. XXV. 10.—

As we have experienced thy readiness to Serve this province on all occasions We before it may be our excuse for this additional trouble from

Let the package for transportation be examined with particular care. and the full value Insured there   Signed by —   Thy Assured Fr'ds
Isaac Norris
Thomas Leech
Edward Warner

Norris' letterbook copy of his order to Robert Charles to "Get us a good bell." *Historical Society of Pennsylvania.*

Partridge was the Crown's representative in Philadelphia; Robert Charles, his assistant, served as spokesman for Pennsylvania in London and as a conveyor of information from the Crown to the Colony. Therefore, the Speaker of the Assembly, Isaac Norris, sent a letter dated November 1, 1751, to London:

by Capt'n Child

RESPECTED FRIEND, ROBERT CHARLES:

The Assembly having ordered us (the Superintendents of our Statehouse) to procure a Bell from England to be purchased for their use we take the Liberty to apply ourselves to thee to get us a good Bell of about two thousand pounds weight the cost of which we presume may amount to about one hundred pounds Sterling or perhaps with the Charges something more and accordingly we have now inclosed a first Bill of Exchange *viz,* John Perrin and Son on Messrs. Thomas Flowerdew & Company for £100 Sterling. We would have chosen to remit a larger Bill at this time, but will take care to furnish more as soon as we can be informed how much may be wanted.

We hope and rely on thy care and assistance in this affair and that thou wilt procure and forward it by the first good opportunity as our workmen inform us it will be much less trouble to hang the Bell before their scaffolds are Struck from the Building where we intend to place it which will not be done 'till the end of next Summer or beginning of the Fall. Let the Bell be cast by the best Workmen and examined carefully before it is Shipped with the following words well shaped in large letters round it *viz:* "By order of the Assembly of the Province of Pensylvania[sic] for the Statehouse in the City of Philadelphia, 1752." and underneath, "Proclaim Liberty thro' all the Land to all the Inhabitants Thereof — Levit. XXV 10."

As we have experienced thy readiness to Serve this Province on all occasions We desire it may be our excuse for this additional trouble from

> Thy Assured Friends
>
> Signed by { ISAAC NORRIS
> THOMAS LEECH
> EDWARD WARNER

Let the package for transportation be examined with particular care and the full value Insured there.

It should be noted that the above letter and those Norris letters which are quoted in the following pages are taken from Norris' own copies, preserved in manuscript form by the Pennsylvania Historical Society. The original documents which Norris sent to Charles are lost and the records of the foundry which cast the Bell were destroyed by a fire late in the nineteenth century as well as by bombings during World War II. This priceless and fascinating letterbook, kept partly in the hand of Norris and partly of two other individuals, probably secretaries, contains the only surviving record of the order for the Bell and Norris' original inscription.

Isaac Norris was the namesake son of a wealthy merchant and public servant who came to Philadelphia from Jamaica in 1692 and prospered. A devout member of the Society of Friends, the elder Norris raised his son accordingly, with emphasis on a superior education. Isaac, Jr., who had gone to school in England for two years when he was six years old, knew Hebrew, Latin and French and was a keen student of the Bible.

When his father died, young Isaac took over his business affairs and soon became active in provincial matters. He became a member of the Provincial Assembly in 1736 and ascended to the Speakership in 1750. He had served as a member or chairman of every important provincial committee and was invariably chosen to conduct the Colony's correspondence with England.

Inherited wealth and his own business acumen enabled him to retire at a relatively early age and from then on devote his life almost totally to the welfare of Pennsylvania. As correspondent to the Crown, he was champion of the civil rights and liberties of his fellow colonials against the usurpation and oppressions of the British King. He fought hard for the things he believed in, especially freedom from English rule, until ill health forced him to resign in 1764. The inscription he ordered placed upon the Bell was no accident; it embodied the principles he, as well as most of his associates, cherished most.

It is doubtful, however, that either Norris or the rest of the Assembly had the slightest inkling of the fateful nature of the prophecy chosen for the Bell. Yet, for their time, no better words could have been found. Penn's *Charter of Privileges,* the final frame of government to be adopted by the "Province of Pennsylvania and Territories thereunto belonging," had indeed brought fifty years of peace, prosperity and civil liberty for the colonists, just as Penn had intended. Leviticus, Chapter XXV, Verse 10, reads:

> And ye shall hallow the fiftieth year, and proclaim liberty throughout *all* the land unto the inhabitants thereof: it shall be a jubilee unto you; and ye shall return every man unto his possession, and ye shall return every man unto his family. [King James translation]

To the Israelites the "Year of the Jubilee" was, in fact, a rebirth of the whole nation, a year in which property was redistributed, slaves freed, debts cancelled and inequalities of the past fifty years removed. Although the Assembly had no intention of cancelling debts or redistributing property, its members were proud to proclaim their fifty years of successful government. Beyond this, however, a second and more far-reaching interpretation can be made.

While Isaac Norris transmitted the Assembly's order for the Bell, it is conceivable that the selection of the passage from Leviticus XXV may have been suggested to Norris by Benjamin Franklin. In mid-eighteenth-century Philadelphia, a city which has been called the "Athens of America," Franklin was its Plato. He wrote profusely on a wide range of subjects, including science, government and social problems. His letters, papers and even his newspaper, the *Pennsylvania Gazette,* contain many Biblical and classical allusions and quotations. Norris' letters, on the other hand, reveal no such scholarly or poetic tones. They are business-like, dedicated and the work of an able statesman — but not of a philosopher.

Most important, however, is the fact that in the year 1751 Franklin was to write two documents which established the foundations for what his biographer, Carl Van Doren, called ". . . a large, new conception of the whole of American life," and which set forth social principles that were to be reflected many times over in Franklin's later political thoughts and actions.

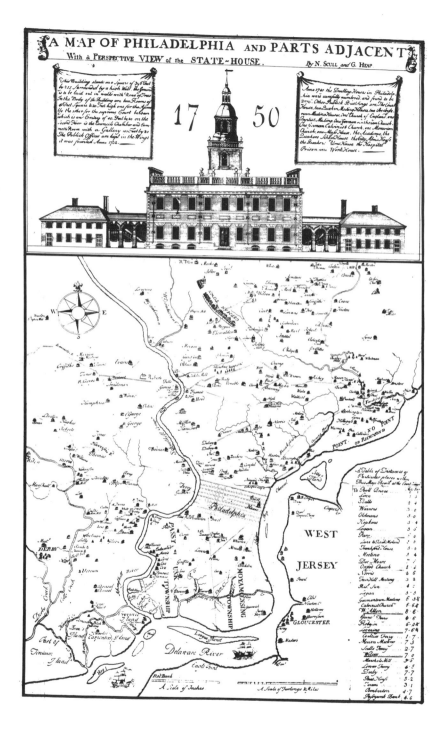

An early glimpse of the concepts that were developing in the mind of this young editor-philosopher appeared in the *Gazette* of May 18, 1749. Extolling the growth of Philadelphia since its founding by William Penn, Franklin first gave a factual census of the city's "Dwelling-Houses" — there were 2076 such buildings, as counted by "twelve careful persons." Then Franklin turned philosopher:

> . . . what a vast improvement have our old men seen. . . . [Penn] has done this by his WISDOM; and has drawn multitudes of people of various Nations, even out of the innermost parts of Europe. . . . Orpheus is said to have built a city by his music . . . but the sweetest of all sounds is LIBERTY; and wholesome Laws with good Government make the most enchanting HARMONY.

By 1751 Franklin was taking a keen interest in Colonial politics and, in March of that year, was to propose a union of the Colonies; ". . . a voluntary Union entered into by the Colonies themselves, I think, would be preferable to one imposed by Parliament." This radical concept culminated in the Albany Conference of 1754 at which Franklin presented his "Plan of Union." But Franklin was too far ahead of his time; the Colonies could not overcome their individual jealousies and separatism, and the Plan was rejected.

It is Franklin's 1751 treatise entitled *Observations Concerning the Increase of Mankind, Peopling of Countries, Etc.* that most clearly points to its author as the man responsible for the Bell's motto. Franklin was at work on this paper during the latter part of 1751, and probably completed it around the same time that the Assembly resolved to order the Bell. He was, it might be added, present in the Assembly chamber the day the resolution was passed, October 16, 1751, according to the minutes of the meeting.

In *Observations* Franklin foresaw with uncanny vision not only the great potential of the American frontier, but the rise of an industrial nation with its tremendous growth in population. And, most important with respect to the Bell's motto, Franklin called upon Britain to keep her hands out of Colonial economic affairs. Instead of restricting Colonial manufacturing of goods as Britain was doing in order to support a rapidly declining market for her own products, she should encourage the growth of "her children." The social concepts Franklin set forth in this document are in some respects strikingly similar to Leviticus, Chapter XXV, and in at least one instance, a direct parallel can be drawn. Franklin wrote: "Foreign Luxuries and needless Manufactures imported and used in a Nation . . . increase the People of the Nation that furnishes them, and diminish the People of the Nation that uses them." Verse 14 of Leviticus XXV reads: "And if thou sell ought unto thy neighbor, or buyest ought of thy neighbor's hand, ye shall not oppress one another."

Thus Franklin, the scholar and philosopher as well as politician, was not only aware of the tenth verse of Leviticus XXV, but at the time the Assembly decided to order its Bell, the theme expressed in this Chapter was on his mind. Could he have seen the opportunity to "proclaim liberty," if merely in an economic sense, to the inhabitants not only of Pennsylvania but of a hoped-for United Colonies? Certainly, as a close friend of Isaac Norris, Franklin had ample opportunity to confer with him and suggest the inscription. Unfortunately, however, no mention of the State House Bell nor its inscription has been found in any of Franklin's letters or papers — and thus the true meaning of the motto to the Assembly of 1751 must remain historical conjecture.

In less than twenty-five years after the ordering of the Bell, a liberty of far greater magnitude would indeed be proclaimed "throughout all the land" and the instrument of proclamation would be the State House Bell itself. But it would not be the same Bell just ordered from London which would sound the call to Revolution — not, at least, until it had been tried by fire; until it bore the unmistakable imprint of American hands and American remolding.

The Casting
of
Bells

I N SPITE OF HIS STATEMENT THAT A £100 BILL OF EXCHANGE WAS enclosed in his letter to Robert Charles, Norris did not actually send the bill until three days later. Presumably, both letters were carried to London on the same ship and received simultaneously by Charles.

The agent lost no time in translating the request into fact. Summoning his carriage, he went to the Sign of the Three Bells in Whitechapel Street and presented his problem to Thomas Lester, Master Founder at the Whitechapel Bell Foundry since 1738. While he shared the title of Master Founder with Thomas Pack, who joined the foundry in 1752, Lester himself chose to supervise the making of the Pennsylvania bell, although subsequent events in its life may have caused him some regret at his decision.

Since bells were the prime means of swift communication in the eighteenth century, the combined art and science of bell making was taken quite seriously, particularly by the British. A fierce pride in workmanship existed, evident in the fact that there are many bells that are still rung today which were cast over four hundred years ago.

29

Whitechapel Bell Foundry today. While modernized inside, the building's exterior looks much the same as it did in the eighteenth century. *Courtesy Whitechapel Bell Foundry.*

If Lester followed standard procedure, he first went to his drafting room and made drawings of the particular design he had in mind for the bell. From these drawings, carefully scaled, the shape and varied thicknesses emerged. The sound, it was said, was already present in the head of the designer. In his design, Lester created the finished drawings using the more or less standard formula as his point of departure.

A bell consists of four distinct parts: the *sound-bow,* which is actually the thick lower lip of the bell and the part the clapper strikes; the *waist,* which is concave and constitutes most of the bell's surface; the *shoulder,* which rises above the waist and usually contains the inscription; and the *crown,* which is the top. *Cannons* or loops are affixed to the crown to suspend the bell from its *yoke.* (Details of the State House Bell are shown on page 48.)

The basic consideration in the design of a bell is the mathematical relationship between its various parts. A bell can be thought of as a succession of metal hoops, each of which produces a different tone that, when sounded together, create a perfect chord. The standard measurements used for most large bells were based upon the thickness of the metal at the sound-bow. The diameter of the bell's mouth was fifteen times this thickness; the height from lip to shoulder was twelve times this thickness; and the diameter at the shoulder 7½ times the thickness, or half the diameter of the mouth. These measurements could be varied by the designer, depending on the exact combination of tones he desired.

Every bell is cast from two molds: the *core* which gives shape to its inner surface, and the *cope* which determines the outer surface. When placed one atop the other, the space in between the two molds forms the bell when filled with molten metal. Simply stated, if you were to invert a flower pot five inches in diameter (the cope) over a flower pot of four-inch diameter (the core), the space between the two pots would, when filled with metal, become a bronze flower pot, its shape and thickness determined by the shapes of the two pots.

With his drawings completed, Lester ordered the making of two *strickle boards* or *crooks*. These boards were wooden templates which were curved to the inner and outer shapes of the bell, respectively. When rotated in a circle around the respective molds, they shaped the inner and outer surfaces intended by the designer for his proposed bell.

Now came the laborious task of casting the bell. The core for the State House Bell was made according to standard procedure. A pit was dug in the ground and within it a brick base, partially hollow to permit the building of a fire, was constructed in the rough shape of the inner surface of the bell. Over this was applied a mixture of yellow London clay, horse manure and soft cow hair mixed with water. The first crook, which had been positioned on a stake through the center of the brick foundation, was rotated around the growing core in the manner of a draftsman's compass until the core reached the exact shape of the crook and had a smooth surface. A charcoal fire was then lit within the hollow part of the brick and the core allowed to harden from the heat.

The second step was to build a clay replica of the bell itself over the solid core. The core was greased, often with pig fat, to prevent sticking and then was wound with one or more layers of straw rope. The second crook was put in the place of the first, and clay was then

Steps in early bell casting. ABOVE: the core is being shaped with a wooden crook. BELOW: a finishing layer of china clay being applied to the inside of the cope.

ABOVE: lowering the cope over the core. BELOW: pouring the metal. All illustrations from Cassel's Magazine of Art, circa 1850. *Courtesy Whitechapel Bell Foundry.*

built up over the rope-covered core until the outer shape of the bell had been achieved. This, in effect created a perfect clay model of the bell. When it had been smoothed with the crook and dried, the clay bell was greased with another layer of pig fat and the thick, outer cope was built up from the same material as the core.

Finally, when the cope was dry, it could be lifted off the clay model of the bell and the model itself broken off the core, leaving only the core and cope molds. The core and the inner surface of the cope were then redressed, smoothed and coated with a fine layer of china clay. If an inscription was to appear on the bell, sections were cut from the inside of the cope at the places where the wording would fall and these openings filled with soft clay. The letters and other markings were then impressed into this in reverse form and the whole cope given a final drying and coating of china clay. The end effect was that of a large china cup that would fit over a smaller one and give the bell its smooth surfaces.

The cope was then lowered back into the pit over the core, lined up exactly, and the pit filled with earth and tightly packed to prevent the cope from bursting or lifting when the hot metal was poured. After the separately made crown with its six cannon loops had been added to the top of the cope, the shape of the bell was complete. Two holes were left in the crown, one for pouring metal into the mold and one to allow the air to escape. A trough was run from the furnace to the hole in the crown, and the molten bell metal — a composition of about 77 per cent copper and 23 per cent tin — flowed in until the mold was filled. The bell was allowed to cool in its subterranean chamber for several days, the exact length of time depending upon its size. When the bell had solidified, the pit was opened, the cope lifted off and the new bell, almost black in color, was revealed for the first time. It was in turn hoisted from its core and made ready for the final step — tuning.

Eighteenth-century bell tuning was a truly fine art which required a good ear and much patience. The finished bell was inverted and pieces of metal were chipped and shaved from the inside until the final tone satisfied the tuner. The two most evident sounds emitted by a bell are the *strike note,* heard on impact of the clapper, and the *hum note* which swells up afterward. Early bell tuners worked primarily with the strike note which, in the case of the State House Bell, was E flat. Once tuned to everyone's satisfaction, the bell was ready for a last polishing and delivery to its belfry.

In the eighteenth century it was customary for town and church dignitaries to attend the pouring of the metal, lending their presence and approval to the bell. It was also a custom to throw gold and silver pieces into the molten metal as it was being poured; it was thought that these precious metals gave added purity to the bell's tone. However, the right proportion of copper and tin had to be maintained to produce the most pleasing tone; the addition of silver or gold added nothing to that tone and might, in fact, cloud it.

The State House Bell very likely entered this world alone and unattended by the customary ritual. It is possible that Robert Charles and Lester, along with workmen, witnessed the pouring, but most certainly there was no Bishop present to annoint or name it. Nor do we know of any Philadelphia dignitaries in attendance to voice solemn approval of design or tone. But the Bell did not need any such pomp or circumstance. Its destiny was already graven on its shoulder and now, having been given life, it simply sat in the dim mustiness of Whitechapel Foundry in its own copper-colored splendor, awaiting passage on the ship that was to take it across the Atlantic to its new home.

It is interesting to note that the same basic process for casting large bells has been used for over six hundred years. Today cast-iron cores have replaced the clay and dung mixture, and mechanically turned lathes and sensitive electronic tuning instruments are in use (although the *final* tone is determined by a human ear). But otherwise, there has been little change in the fine art of bell casting.

Whitechapel's "Sign of the Three Bells" as used today.

One of Robert Mot's early bells cast by him at Whitechapel Foundry in 1573 for Dagnam Hall, Essex, England. *London Museum.*

Two
Ingenious
Workmen

N O RECORD SURVIVES OF ANY PROPOSED DELIVERY DATE FOR the Bell, but certainly its arrival could not be expected until the following year. When 1752 reached midpoint, however, Norris found himself wondering when the Bell would appear. On August 9, a bit more than nine months after placing his order, he wrote Charles inquiring about some glass for the State House windows as well as other pertinent matters and added, almost apologetically, a postscript to his letter:

P.S. We are looking for the Bell daily —
I have given R. Partridge orders to discharge
your balance. . . .

Norris' patience was rewarded sooner than he expected. Within a short while after his letter departed for London, a ship sailed slowly up the Delaware bearing the long awaited cargo. While historians have conjectured that the honored vessel was the *Myrtilla* under the command of Captain Richard Budden, Philadelphia's port entry

Cast at Whitechapel Foundry in 1757, the bell of St. Paul's Church, Mount Vernon, N.Y., shows the original yoke, frame and ringing wheel which accompanied it on its voyage to America. Although only one-fourth of the size of the State House Bell, the St. Paul's bell illustrates a complete eighteenth-century bell structure. *Courtesy St. Paul's Church.*

records published in the *Pennsylvania Gazette* show the *Myrtilla's* arrival as the week of September 21, at least three weeks after Norris says the Bell came ashore.

However, the *Pennsylvania Journal,* published in Philadelphia by William Bradford, reveals a clue not only to the identity of the ship, but to a possible cause of damage to the bell while in transit. In the August 27 issue is the notation: "Tuesday arrived here Capt'n Child in the *Hibernia* from London in 11 weeks." The same issue contains a remark about "recent storms which have plagued us. . . ." Since the *Hibernia* was the only cargo-carrying vessel to arrive near the end of August and eleven weeks was a longer than average passage from London to Philadelphia, one can surmise that the Bell had a rough voyage to America — aboard the same ship that had carried its order from Norris to Charles the previous year!

Norris was far too busy a man to be concerned with the physical problems of a bell beyond keeping informed of its progress. The details of the unloading, assembly and preparations for raising were probably left to Edmund Woolley, who had charge of the State House construction. Norris was not present to witness the Bell's arrival nor the first trial — and resultant catastrophe. He did, however, keep Robert Charles up-to-date, and on September 1, 1752, wrote:

The bell is come ashore & in good order & we hope it will prove a good one for I have heard that it is approved by all hitherto, tho we have not yet tryd the sound. . . . The superintendents of the State House by me return their thanks for thy care in procuring us so good a bell and we may hereafter join in a letter for that purpose.

If the usual procedure for transportation and delivery of large bells had been followed, the Great Bell arrived in the ship's hold carefully packed with its frame, yoke, ringing wheel and clapper ready to assemble and hoist into the steeple. Woolley may have ordered his men to load the Bell onto a wagon at the dock and cart it directly to the State House yard, although Norris does not indicate the actual place where disaster was soon to strike.

The scene, however, is easy to visualize. When the heavy load reached its destination, the natural curiosity of all concerned to hear its tone must have been considerable. Undoubtedly a formal raising ceremony was being planned, but before this took place, why not hang the Bell on a temporary stand and test it? Woolley may well have erected the Bell's frame on the ground, mounted the yoke to the Bell, and hoisted the whole unit into place on the frame.

Now, with the Bell suspended a few feet above the ground, the clapper was bolted inside to the crown. Then some luckless, unnamed individual — perhaps Woolley himself — grasped the heavy clapper, drew it to him, and sent it flying toward the opposite edge of the brim. A loud bong came forth, followed by a discordant hum as the Bell quivered and reverberated. No sooner had the clapper struck than the horrified man and his companions watched a crack split the brim. How far into the Bell it raced is left unsaid, but the extent of damage was great enough to render the Whitechapel Bell totally useless — on its first stroke in the New World.

Several causes of this catastrophe have been advanced in the years since then. Norris, who waited until March 10, 1753, to inform Robert Charles of the events, placed the blame on Whitechapel, stating that ". . . our judges have generally agreed that [the metal] was too high & brittle. . . ." When Lester received this news, he was shocked by the inference that the crack was the result of inferior production. From that day forward, Whitechapel has insisted that the cracking was caused by an "amateur bell-ringer" who, being unknowledgeable in the ways of bells, may have held the clapper against the brim after striking it, and the resultant vibration caused the metal to split. Regardless of who tested the Bell or how it was done, it now seems clear that the *Hibernia* was tossed about on stormy seas and the Bell could have suffered a blow at least severe enough to cause a fracture in its brittle metal. When struck with the clapper, this small crack would spring open and result in irreparable damage. Assuming this to be the case, Whitechapel can be absolved of the blame once and for all.

Today Whitechapel tells anybody who is interested that the Pennsylvania Bell is the *only* product of the company to crack in testing in over four hundred years. Mr. Douglas Hughes, Master Founder and one of the present co-owners of Whitechapel Foundry, further explained their position in a letter dated September 20, 1972, stating that it is quite obvious Norris and his "judges" were "unaware that the essential quality in bell metal is its brittleness, for without this, a bell will not ring."

The exact happenings that day of the fatal cracking probably will never be known — only some hitherto undiscovered letter or diary could reveal the facts. But nevertheless, the Bell was unusable, and something had to be done. Norris, in his letter to Charles of March 10, 1753, some six months later, gives only a brief clue to what was to follow:

> . . . our Bell was generally liked & approved of but in a few days after my writing [September 1, 1752] I had the mortification to hear that it was cracked by the stroke of the clapper without any other viollence [*sic*] as it was hung up to try the sound . . . we concluded to send it back by Captain Budden but he could not take it on board upon which two Ingenious Work-Men undertook to cast it here. . . .

It was a natural response on the part of Norris and the Assembly to send the faulty merchandise back to Whitechapel. Captain Budden was advertising weekly in the *Pennsylvania Gazette* beginning September 28 that ". . . the ship *Myrtilla* will sail on or before the last of October, having a great part of her cargo ready. . . ." Thus, when Norris inquired of Budden if he would take back the heavy Bell, the Captain refused because his ship was already too full.

The most fascinating aspect of the letter quoted above is the reference to "two Ingenious Work-Men," who, in a letter dated April 14, 1753, Norris further identified as ". . . a native of the Isle of Malta and a son of Charles Stow." Until now their qualifications to recast a two-thousand-pound bell have remained a mystery which, in turn, gave rise to the legend that they were amateurs with a tremendous amount of ingenuity. Close examination of Edmund Woolley's meticulously kept account books, the issues of the *Gazette* of that period, and other records, has shed considerable light on the identity of at least one of the members of the "Pass and Stow" team.

On October 16, 1752, the Pennsylvania Assembly adjourned to the "fifteenth of January next" after having unanimously re-elected Isaac Norris its Speaker, and Woolley was left in charge of doing something

For *JAMAICA, directly,*
The *Brigantine*
CUMBERLAND,
JOHN LOWNES,
Commander;
Will sail with all expedition, having great part of her cargoe already engaged. For freight or passage, agree with said master, on board said vessel, lying at White Massey's wharff. ¶

JOHN STOW, Brass-Founder,
Is remov'd from Third-street, to the sign of the Three Bells, in Second-street, opposite to Mr. John Lawrence's, and next door but two to Mr. William Whitebread's, at the sign of the King's Arms, Philadelphia;

WHere may be had, all sorts of brasses suitable for the West-India sugar-mills, grist-mills, saw-mills, &c. brass furniture of every sort for coaches, chaises, &c. brass fire-dogs, shovel and tongs, candlesticks, gun-furniture, best brass shoe-buckles, and sleeve-buttons, by the quantity or single pair, joiners furniture of several sorts, spoon-moulds, of all fashions, bell-metal skillets and kettles, of all sizes, ditto mortars and pestles, house spring-bells, of all sizes, ditto for horses, copper rivets and brass cocks for stills, of all sizes, barrel cocks, dog-collars, brass heads for iron dogs, of all sizes, brass stirrups, saddle heads and nails, knockers for doors, with a variety of other brass work, at the most reasonable rates. Likewise work in the rough, for clock-makers, &c.

To be Sold by ANDREW REED,
Next door to the Jersey Ferry, in Water-Street,

WEst-India rum, New-England ditto, cocoa, chocolate, oil, flints, bar lead, muscovado sugar in barrels, corks, dripping pans of several sizes, choice good Jesuits bark, very good Trenton pork and beef, gammons loose, ditto pack'd in barrels, ship-bread pack'd, or in bulk, pickled cod in barrels, good Rhode-Island cheese, hogshead and pipe staves, and hogshead heading. ¶

John Stow's advertisement in the *Pennsylvania Gazette,* April 16, 1752. *New York Public Library, Rare Book Division.*

about the cracked Bell. Being a skilled craftsman, Woolley at first tried to repair the damage himself and, on October 24, recorded in his account book the purchase of "a large file, for the cracked bell . . . £ 0/2/6." But filing the crack failed to salvage the Bell; and Woolley, a master craftsman himself, turned to the most expert help he could find — John Stow, a Philadelphia brass founder.

Stow was the only person at the time to advertise the manufacture of brass products in Philadelphia; no ads appeared for bell founders. There were, however, several bell founders in New England, including some who offered to cast bells as large as "Two Thousand Weight." As early as June of 1717, one Joseph Phillips, who was establishing himself as a bell founder in New York, ran the following notice in the *Boston News-Letter,* an item that is strikingly ironic in light of the cracked Great Bell thirty-five years later:

BELL FOUNDER — This is to give notice to all Persons that have occasion for a Bell or Bells in Churches or Meeting-houses, that in New York they may be supplyed with New Bells, or if they have any old Bell broke they may have it new cast at a reasonable Price, and warranted good for Twelve Months, that if it Crack or Break it shall be new Cast for nothing: And all New Bells shall be made of better metal than any other that comes out of Europe for Churches or Meeting-houses. All Persons that have Occasion may apply themselves to Joseph Phillips who is now building a Furnace for that purpose, and hath already agreed with some Persons, and is ready to do the same with any that are disposed.

It is unlikely that Woolley would permit the recasting of so large a bell by someone without experience; the task was a formidable one which certainly could not be undertaken by an amateur, no matter how "ingenious" he might be. By March of 1752, John Stow had moved his foundry from Third Street to "the Sign of the Three Bells, in Second-Street. . . ," a location close by the State House. In this sign lies a clue for believing that John Stow not only knew bell casting, but could have learned the trade in England, perhaps even at Whitechapel itself.

The London foundry had been established in 1570 by Robert Mot on Whitechapel Road, just across from the site of the present foundry. Over his door hung a sign showing three gold bells, making his address in those days of numberless streets "at the sign of the three bells in Whitechapel Street." This same mark was in use in 1752, and is still the Whitechapel trademark today. So far as can be determined, the "three bells" symbol was used by only two foundries — Whitechapel of London and John Stow of Philadelphia. It is difficult to draw any other conclusion than that Stow at least knew of Whitechapel and from sentiment, as well as appreciation of the quality of the London firm, adopted its symbol for his own foundry. Mr. Douglas Hughes confirms this theory and in a letter of April 1, 1973, stated: ". . . one cannot but assume that Stow got the idea of his sign from our use of it at Whitechapel. It was not a common sign."

Further evidence of Stow's ability can be seen in the wide variety of products he offered. Almost every imaginable household item is included from brass furniture to rivets, but beyond these he specified ". . . all sorts of brasses suitable for the West-India sugar-mills, grist-mills, saw-mills, etc." Stow was not only a local brass merchant; he was an exporter of brass products to other Colonies as well. Although the only bells he advertised were "house spring-bells, ditto for horses," he was clearly a man who knew the brass foundry trade.

But who was the "Pass" of the famous team of Pass and Stow? Unfortunately, little is known of his identity except that he was a native of Malta and that his first name was John. However, on the reverse of the bill submitted by Pass and Stow for their services, the two men signed in receipt of payment — Stow signed his name as "John Stowe" and Pass placed an "X" in the space left for "John Pass — his mark." Thus, Pass probably could not write; whether he could read is open to question. No further use of the trade name "Pass and Stow" has been found, nor has any other trace of John Pass been uncovered. Could Stow have hired Pass as an assistant and complimented him by the inclusion of his name on the Bell? Or was Pass himself a skilled founder? We shall probably never know.

At
the Sign
of the Three Bells

W ITH THE APPARENT KNOWLEDGE AND SKILL NEEDED FOR
bell casting, the fate of the Bell now rested squarely on
John Pass and John Stow. After being informed of the
decision, the two founders took the Bell from its temporary rigging
and carted it off to their foundry.

There is no record of the exact technique used by the men as they
tackled the monumental job. It is safe to assume, however, that their
method at least approximated that used by Whitechapel and other
bell foundries, and would be the same if Stow had learned bell casting
in England. Probably they first molded a core and a cope from the
Whitechapel Bell before melting it down, a move that would have
been not only practical but necessary to guarantee that the new Bell
would be a twin of the first.

Once the core and cope were finished, the old Bell had to be
broken up into small pieces which would fit into the furnace and
would melt with reasonable speed. To achieve the fragmented pile of
metal, the proud Bell had to be sledge-hammered into bits and pieces,
until it was reduced to a heap of rubble on the foundry floor.

"The Bell's First Note" by J. L. G. Ferris. *National Park Service.*

And now they were ready for their venture into bell making. But before applying the fires, they melted down a few pieces of the battered metal and cast several small bells in order to try the sound and strength of the end product. Deciding that more copper was needed, they added, according to Norris, "one ounce and a half for each pound of the old bell." If this was done, about 190 pounds of new metal were given to the composition. Curiously, however, in their statement for work done, Pass and Stow charged for "37 lb. additional weight." In any event, the Assembly members periodically braved the cold Philadelphia winter afternoons to visit the foundry and check the progress. Apparently Isaac Norris was again absent, this time from the unmolding ceremony, for in his letter of March 10 to Robert Charles he continues:

> . . . I am just now informed that they have this day opened the mould, and have got a good bell, which I confess pleases me very much that we should first venture upon and succeed in the greatest bell cast, for ought I know, in English America. The mould was finished in a very masterly manner and the letters, I am told, are better than in the old one.

In the period between March 10 and March 29, however, Pass and Stow's Bell was tested, probably while hanging from a framework in their foundry. Its sound brought second thoughts to the minds of those who heard it and Norris wrote on the 29th to one James Wright:

> . . . Ed Woolley this day has begun to raise the Belfry in order to hang the Bell so that its likely when thou comes down, thou may hear the sound thereof and judge for thyself, for the People seem divided about the Goodness or badness thereof, and it is to be hung in order that every Body may hear & Judge — that is Every Body who has any vote — whether it shall remain or be recast. . . .

Even though the status of the Bell was already in doubt, it was decided to proceed with plans for a feast to celebrate the raising, according to a custom prevalent in England. It was the least the citizenry could do to honor the Bell, and a good cause for a party. Woolley was placed in charge of the gala occasion and he ordered a peck of potatoes, fourteen pounds of beef, four gammons (cured hams) weighing a total of thirty-eight pounds, quantities of mustard, pepper, salt and butter, a thirteen-pound cheese, thirty pounds of beef, and another peck of potatoes at a price, oddly enough, slightly different from the first peck. Lacy, "ye baker," provided thirty-six loaves of bread, Ducher supplied earthenware and candles and a charge was made for cooking and wood. For liquid refreshment, three hundred limes were obtained and one John Jones produced three gallons of rum to make a punch. To top it off, Anthony Morris wheeled a barrel of beer into the State House yard and the feast was ready. The bill, submitted by Woolley on April 17, came to five pounds, thirteen shillings and ten pence.

The Bell, which had been raised by Woolley and his men through trap doors in the various levels of the bell tower, now hung in its frame, all in readiness to be "Judged . . . by Every Body who has a vote. . . ." Democracy, though limited to men of property, was already at work in America — and its vote was negative. Instead of giving forth a melodious sound, the Bell issued a disturbing "bonk" which one irreverent witness described as being somewhat like the sound of

THE STATE HOUSE BELL
(Now the Liberty Bell)

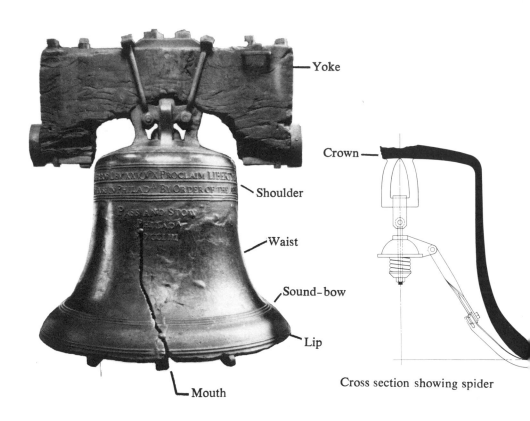

— Yoke

Crown—

— Shoulder

— Waist

— Sound-bow

— Lip

— Mouth

Cross section showing spider

MEASUREMENTS OF THE LIBERTY BELL:

Circumference at lip	12 feet
Circumference at crown	7 feet, 6 inches
Height, lip to crown	3 feet
Length of clapper	3 feet, 2 inches
Thickness at lip	3 inches
Thickness at crown	1¼ inches
Weight of the Bell	2080 pounds

two coal scuttles banged together. Pass and Stow's embarrassment was heightened even more by the "witticisms," as Norris tactfully put it, hurled at them by the spectators. They were so "tiezed," Norris wrote, that they immediately began preparations for a second recasting. On April 14, Norris described the debacle briefly to Robert Charles:

> . . . they made the Mould in a Masterly Manner and run the metal well, but upon tryal, it seems they added too much copper in the present bell which is now hung up in its place . . . and will be very soon ready to make a second essay — if this should fail, we will embrace Lister's [*sic*] offer and send the unfortunate Bell to him by first opportunity.

While Woolley — and probably Norris and other members of the Assembly — sat disconsolately mulling the challenge of the Bell, John Pass and John Stow apparently went onto a twenty-four-hour-a-day schedule, working feverishly to produce the second recasting or, to be precise, the third Bell. The frenzy of their pace is evident in the fact that by the first week of June the Bell was once again hung in the steeple. The *Pennsylvania Gazette,* which so far had not taken notice of the events that were to achieve such fame in history, mentioned the final hanging in its issue of June 7, 1753:

> Last week was raised and fix'd in the Statehouse Steeple, the new great Bell, cast here by Pass and Stow, weighing 2080 lb with this Motto, *Proclaim Liberty throughout all the Land unto all the Inhabitants thereof; Lev. XXV 10.*

That same week the Assembly adjourned until the following August and this time there was no celebration on the part of the public. But the bell hangers partook, for in Woolley's ledger sheets is the entry "Victuals & drink 4 days for John Baker and ye hanging the Bell." The Bell may still have had its problems, for "a gill of oyl & Bottle, for the Bell" was purchased on May 29. Woolley, in his final itemized statement for the erection of the bell tower, included charges for ". . . getting the Bell up & down & up again & twice hanging bells. . . ." On July 3, Pass and Stow submitted their bill and on July 11 were paid sixty pounds, thirteen shillings and five pence. The Great Bell that was eventually to become the Liberty Bell had found its place — and it stayed.

The inscription on the final Bell was changed slightly in physical appearance, although not in content, from the wording found on Norris' letterbook copy of his order for the Bell. Certain words and characters were abbreviated: "Levit." became "Lev." and a peculiar conjunction of the letters "v" and "s" served to signify "verse." Where Norris had incorrectly used the words "thro" and "to" in the Biblical quotation, Pass and Stow followed their Bible and engraved them as "throughout" and "unto." In addition, the words "in the City of" preceding "Philadelphia" were deleted. Since no record exists to show the actual inscription on the first Bell that arrived from Whitechapel, we can never know who actually made these changes. Possibly Robert Charles extracted the quotation from Norris' letter and made some alterations and corrections before passing the wording on to Whitechapel. Or perhaps the founders, while adding the Pass and Stow imprint, altered the inscription. One can only conjecture about this small point of history.

The most notable feature in the Bell's inscription as it now stands, however, is the spelling of the word "Pennsylvania" with one "n." As the inset from Norris' letterbook shows, the single "n" was present in the copy and thus may well have been in the original. From here one can imagine the error being carried to Whitechapel's Bell and then passing unnoticed in the recastings. Certainly Pass and Stow can be absolved of the blame for originating such a mistake and may be accused only of not correcting it.

Although the Bell was now serving its purpose in the State House tower, Isaac Norris still had misgivings about its sound. On November 8, 1753, he wrote Robert Charles that ". . . tho' some are of the opinion it will do, I Own I do not like it . . ." and requested him to order a second bell from Whitechapel as soon as possible. When that was received, Norris reasoned, the first Bell could be sent back for credit against the second and in the meantime the State House would have a Bell to call its members to session, regardless of how melodious its ring.

In the spring of 1754 the new bell arrived, but John Stow was never to hear the sound of his competition; he died on March 15. Norris wrote in May, however, that no decision had been made regarding the return of the first Bell for credit because " . . . the difference in comparing them is not very good." The problem was finally ended by a resolution of the Assembly early in August:

RESOLVED: That the said Superintendent do pay for the new Bell, and keep the old one for such uses as this House may hereafter appoint.

In the same session the Assembly, without even a single debate, voted against adoption of the Plan of Confederation drawn up at Albany, rejecting, as did all other Colonies except New York, this first move toward a united Colonies. But they did save the Great Bell for a union to come two decades later.

It is likely that the second Whitechapel bell was a duplicate of the first because Norris, in his letter to Charles of November 8, requested that it be made under terms formerly proposed by Lester, namely "two pence a pound for recasting." The accounts of the Province of Pennsylvania show that monies relating to the first Bell and paid at various times to Isaac Norris amounted to £198, which sum probably represented the ultimate cost of the first Whitechapel Bell. An entry in the ledger of the Committee of Accounts for August 15, 1754, however, records payment of £170, and notes it as "paid to Isaac Norris for Robert Charles, towards a bell." The

Enlargement from Norris' letter and the inscription on the Bell showing the misspelled "Pensylvania."

difference in the costs of the two London bells might indicate that the second was smaller than the first, and so cost less. However, if the original core and cope of the first casting had been saved, the cost of their construction could have been deducted from the price of the second bell, and thus account for the lower figure.

Almost immediately, the American Bell in the tower became known by the legislators' designation as "The Old One," and thus achieved a kind of instant antiquity. It was never attached to the clock. Instead, "The Other One" — the second English bell — was quietly hung in a new cupola or turret jutting from the State House roof just in front of the tower, where it eventually tolled the hours for Penn's colonists. (One source says it was not hung *in* the turret, but placed next to it on the roof.) "The Old One," quite obviously, was reserved for more exciting purposes.

The function of the English bell is not clear during the period from 1754 to 1759; it was not until the latter year that it was attached to the clock and began its hourly tolling. In 1828, the English cousin and its clock were donated to St. Augustine's Roman Catholic Church on Fourth Street, below Vine. There it suffered a tragic fate. In May, 1844, when the anti-Catholic Native American riots erupted in Philadelphia, the Church was burned to the ground and the bell was badly damaged. Fragments of it were recovered, however, and recast into another bell which is now at Villanova University.

In a roundabout way the State House Bell went into action almost at once to warrant its prophetic inscription by freeing at least one Philadelphian from "oppression." With Pass and Stow doubtless held in great esteem by the citizens of Philadelphia after their successful recasting of the Bell, it is possible that John Stow's father was spurred into action on an old problem he had long endured. Charles Stow, who was Doorkeeper of the Assembly, also acted as a supplier to the Mayor's Court. On July 23, 1753, with his son's success providing courage, he went to the City Council and demanded payment for "Firewood and Candles, supplied by him at the Mayor's Court for Two and Twenty years past." The demand was met and "The Board agreed to allow him seven shillings and six pence per annum for the said fire and Candles and His trouble relating thereunto."

The Years
Before
Liberty

THE STATE HOUSE BELL, PERCHED IN ITS LOFTY STEEPLE, WAS called upon to perform its first official duty on the afternoon of August 27, 1753, when the Assembly reconvened. Having been cast "at the Sign of the Three Bells," a strange coincidence in view of the three bells, the last of which would become the famed Liberty Bell a century later, the Great Bell was also surrounded by other remarkable coincidences. First of all, it was housed in a building for which ground had been broken in 1732, the year in which George Washington had been born. The Bell itself bore the prophetic inscription which heralded the coming Revolution, the instrument which would enable the founding fathers of this brash young nation to "proclaim Liberty throughout all the land." And now, it rang for the first time to call the Pennsylvania Assembly together to pass one of the early acts of rebellion that reflected the humor of the people and the growing, if still nebulous, desire to break ties with England. The resolution was a decision to continue issuance of their own currency in direct disobedience to the orders set forth by the Crown.

Having thus begun its life in a climate of anticipation and preparedness, the Bell settled into a relatively mundane existence for the next decade or more, resigned to Philadelphia's blistering summers and biting winters.

In the prosperous, though somewhat uneasy years preceding the Revolution, the Bell looked down from its tower on a bustling, growing city. In 1753, the year the Bell was hung, Philadelphia's population stood at 14,563. By 1776, it was just under thirty thousand, but a census ordered by General Howe in 1777, the year the British occupied the city, found only about fifteen thousand citizens in residence. Clearly, those sympathetic to the Revolution had fled in large numbers. In a few short years, however, a tragic reversal of that flight would occur when beleaguered Tories, persecuted unceasingly by the victors, would be forced to leave the Colonies. Before the exodus was over, more than one hundred thousand British sympathizers living in the Thirteen Colonies would return to England or flee to Canada or the West Indies.

The State House yard encompassed the entire block bounded by Fifth and Sixth streets on the east and west, and by Chestnut and Walnut streets on the north and south. Beyond it new houses were being built at a rapid pace and Philadelphia was sprawling away from its seventeenth-century boundaries. The waterfront was expanding and the city's importance as a Colonial port was already established.

Indians were still part of the passing scene and they mingled from time to time with the grandly dressed ladies and gentlemen who promenaded along Chestnut Street. Indians sometimes stayed in the west wing of the State House, or in nearby sheds which provided quarters for transients. Those who visited or lived within the city were peaceable enough, but tales of Indian atrocities against settlers in the western and northern sections of the province came in with disturbing frequency.

The vague uneasiness which marked the relationship between Crown and Colonies continued, but open hostility was still some distance off. The Assembly, while concerned with matters relating to the conduct of law and business in the province, could also become severely nettled by its own internal problems. In 1755, a sharply worded directive was ordered by the Assembly to its members in an effort to combat absenteeism — a condition which has plagued deliberative and legislative bodies through the ages. The Bell figured largely in the drama of the absent and tardy members. The Bell, it was reasoned, was tolled to call the Assembly together. No one could offer the excuse that he couldn't hear it; all members lived close by the State House, so it followed that each could be in his seat within thirty minutes of the Bell's ring. And so a resolution was introduced — and passed — that "those members who do not appear in the House within half an hour after the Assembly Bell ceases to ring, shall pay one shilling."

It's highly probable that the resolution was suggested, and possibly even drafted, by Isaac Norris, the Bell's prime proponent. A similar resolution decrying tardiness had been on the Assembly's books since 1704, but the members paid little heed to it. Perhaps Norris reasoned that the booming of the great bronze Bell would bring the reluctant Assemblymen into line.

If that were so, Norris was doomed to disappointment. The new resolution was generally ignored, as was the same resolution when readopted the following year. It took four years for patience to wear thin and in February, 1760, a new resolution, hopefully more enforceable, was framed. It read:

RESOLVED, that every member who shall be absent from the House (except on Mondays) longer than Half an Hour after the Bell ceases to ring in the Fore and Afternoon, shall be subject to a fine of One Shilling for every such delinquency and that Mr. Pearce is hereby appointed and empowered to collect the said Fines, for the use of the Pennsylvania Hospital.

The maddening, frustrating behavior of the members who chose to pay their fines rather than appear on time led to an even stiffer penalty. From October 15, 1763, any late or absent member would have to pay two shillings and eight pence for every hour's absence, unless, of course, he could show just cause. That this fine was no deterrent is also evident; one year later the fine was upped to two shillings, *eighteen* pence.

The shocking explosion of the Revolution apparently cured tardiness and absenteeism almost completely. The conscientious and concerned Assembly members faithfully attended all of the somber meetings called when deliberation was necessary. The fine was reduced to fifteen shillings and ultimately dropped when the Assembly was forced to flee to Lancaster during Howe's occupation of Philadelphia.

During the 1750s the Bell continued to send out its peal and perhaps its most significant ring was heard on February 3, 1757, when, in ominous foreboding of the times, it called the Assembly together to direct "Mr. Franklin" to "go home to England" and there recount the numerous grievances of the colonists.

In 1759, the problem of selecting a new bell ringer and Doorkeeper arose. Since its hanging in 1753, the Bell had had two official ringers (who probably also doubled as Doorkeepers). The first, Edward Kelley, sounded the State House Bell from 1753 to 1755. He was replaced by David Edward, who held the post until 1758. For reasons unrecorded, Mr. Edward left his post and it became necessary to name a successor. Since the Doorkeeper-Bellringer was responsible directly to the Speaker of the Assembly, selection of Edward's replacement probably became the responsibility of Isaac Norris. In any case, the record shows that a Mr. Andrew McNair was appointed sometime in 1759 and served the Assembly until 1777, when he was succeeded by William Hurrie. For many years the issue of just who rang the Bell when the Declaration of Independence was read was somewhat clouded. Hurrie was credited by some but the confusion was cleared when diligent research demonstrated that only McNair could have been the bell ringer on that epic day.

Little is known of McNair except that he was a Mason and discharged his duties faithfully. No record of his death or place of burial has been found, perhaps because many records relating to the city and its people were destroyed when the British occupied Philadelphia. The remaining records do show, however, that McNair received compensation ranging from thirty-five to forty pounds a year, and also monies for "other services." In addition, his income was supplemented by payments for Indian wards who were placed in his care by the city. Special occasions when the Bell was "borrowed" by groups other than the Assembly brought further fees.

McNair truly had a comfortable post; following the custom, he and his wife Mary probably made their living quarters in the Bell Tower of the State House.

While the honor of ringing the Bell must go to McNair, it should be pointed out that he might possess that honor by mild default. The Second Continental Congress was in session for 148 days during 1776 and its records show that McNair was actually paid for 146 days of attendance. While one of his two absent days could have been the day on which the Declaration was proclaimed, there is no record of a substitute being called in for the occasion. And so it must remain that McNair was the privileged bell ringer on that first day of independence.

The decade of the 1760s saw the French and Indian War culminating in the French ceding all of Canada to the British and all territories west of the Mississippi to Spain. But the British were to find little peace; while the French were no longer a problem, unrest in the American Colonies gathered greater momentum with each passing year. Relations between Crown and Colonies were balanced on a kind of tight rope, and the Patriots played the game by showing deference and honor to the Mother Country while at the same time protesting loudly over the brand of government, with its attendant rules and regulations, imposed by the British.

The first officially documented ringing of the Bell in the 1760s was on February 21, 1761, when it rang to proclaim the accession of King George III to the English throne. After that, nearly all its recorded rings were sounded in the context of trouble, discontent or dissatisfaction with Britain.

The Bell rang joyfully on January 26, 1763, to announce the end of the French and Indian War; hostilities had ended in 1760, but now the preliminary Treaty of Fountainbleau wrote the final chapter to the seven-year struggle for possession of a great part of America and Canada.

In March of 1764, the Chancellor of the British Exchequer, George Grenville, presented the British House of Commons with the "American Revenue Act," the first in a series of acts designed for the express purpose of raising monies for the Crown, and it passed with little debate. The act quickly became known more familiarly in

America as the "Sugar Act." Its implications were broad and, to the colonists, seemed calculated to destroy their economy. The first resounding protest went up from Massachusetts on May 24. In a town meeting called to display their anger, the now immortal phrase "taxation without representation" was born. The Massachusetts House of Representatives authorized correspondence with the other provinces to inform them of their displeasure and, on September 12, 1764, the Bell rang out loud and clear to summon a meeting of the Pennsylvania Assembly. The Assembly was told of Massachusetts' protest letter to London and commenced its own debate calling for a similar demand for repeal. A few days later, the Bell rang again and the Assembly met for the purpose of drafting a letter patterned after that of Massachusetts.

The gravity of both the Sugar Act and the firm protests it evoked evidently gave much pause for thought in the Pennsylvania Assembly. A little more than a month after it had sent its letter to London, the Assembly decided that Pennsylvania needed personal representation in Britain by a Colonial. The Bell again pealed when, on October 26, 1764, Benjamin Franklin, Esq., departed for London as an ambassador to "transact the affairs of the Province."

By the following year the seeds of revolution had not only been planted, but the first shoots had begun to appear. Now the language of revolution emerged. In his famed "Liberty Speech," the fiery Patrick Henry warned King George III to note the fate of Caesar and Charles I. Secret organizations such as the "Sons of Liberty" were formed and took to violent acts to illustrate their displeasure with Britain. This new unrest and aggressive action came about because of the passage of the Stamp Act in 1765. This act placed taxes on an enormous number of items and the monies therefrom were supposed to be used for the defense of the Colonies. In a rather weak effort to ameliorate the situation, the English appointed Americans to be stamp agents.

While the Stamp Act had been passed in England during February and March, it did not become effective until November 1, 1765. In September, with Massachusetts as the driving force, the Stamp Act Congress was called into session at Federal Hall in New York City. It was composed of representatives from most of the Colonies (four provinces failed to send delegates) and its purpose was to consider means of seeking relief from the loathsome tithings. The Stamp Act Congress took a somewhat moderate stand on the subject and proceeded with resolutions of condemnation, drawing up petitions of protest that were to be submitted to England.

Most effective in fighting the act, however, were the merchants' economic sanctions imposed against imported goods in New York, Boston and Philadelphia. These sanctions led almost directly to the repeal of the Stamp Act in 1766.

1765 had been a busy year for the Bell. It rang on September 9 to call the Assembly together to consider the implications of and possible actions against the Stamp Act. The mighty sadness of the Americans was reflected when, on October 5, the Bell was muffled and rang mournfully to proclaim news of ships proceeding up the Delaware bearing stamps to be used in the execution of the hated act. The ship *Royal Charlotte* bore the stamps and was escorted by British warships. Its final recorded peal for the year occurred October 31 on the eve of the day the Stamp Act took effect. Following this doleful sounding, a group of citizens gathered at Philadelphia's London Coffee House and with great ceremony publicly burned Stamp Act documents.

The only recorded ringing of the Bell during 1766 came on September 30 when, in a session presumably marked by debate that could only have been described as "heated," the Assembly voted four thousand pounds for the King's use. This was the last occasion on which monies would be voted to the King; from this point on, the Bell rang only in a Revolutionary voice.

While there is no official record of the sounding of the Bell on the repeal of the Stamp Act, it seems unlikely that such a momentous victory would not be marked by a pealing from the State House. The act was no longer in force after May 1, 1766, and word of its abolition was received in the Colonies a month later "with rejoicing." Thus it seems fair enough, in spite of the lack of record, that the Bell took part in that celebration.

The following year, 1767, saw more affronts from the Crown through the Townshend Acts, a series of prohibitions which struck directly at the heart of the Colonial economy in enormous measure, and finally in 1768, drew a massive protest meeting at the State House. The Bell was rung to bring together the merchants of the city for the purpose of enumerating grievances of the people resulting from these prohibitions. From the nature of the Parliamentary Acts, it would seem that the merchants were more than a little justified in expressing their annoyance. The new dictums placed import duties on many necessary items and arbitrarily forbade the provinces from making steel or iron, operating planing mills, or manufacturing wool, woolen products and hats. Transporting goods from colony to colony was also forbidden. Clearly, the King was determined to keep the Colonies separate and force them to depend on British imports, but it was just as clear that the Americans were not intending to sit still for such tactics.

That the unrest which had gradually spread through the Colonies was coming dangerously close to boiling over is seen in the next recorded ringing of the Bell. Obviously conditions were growing more and more unpleasant and, on July 30, 1768, the Bell once again called the citizens together "to consider instructions to our representatives in the present critical condition of these Colonies."

By 1770, the language of the Americans in voicing displeasure at the Crown became decidedly more outspoken. On September 22, the Bell summoned a meeting which was marked by "statements" rather than "considerations." At that meeting, the people "resolved that the claims of Parliament to tax the Colonies were subversive of their constitutional rights; that the union of the Colonies ought to be maintained; that everyone who imported goods into the city contrary to these resolutions was an enemy to the peace and good order of the city." This indicated a definite change of climate; now, the colonists were not "considering" this or that injustice — they were telling the Crown how it was.

Whether the Bell rang on the occasion of the Boston Massacre is moot; more than likely it did not. The Boston incident was then considered a minor one and did not achieve notoriety until it was used a few years later by Samuel Adams as an argument for bringing the Revolution into actuality. But the Bell did ring on February 4, 1771, when the Assembly was called together for the express purpose of petitioning the King for repeal of the tax on tea, the commodity destined to play a large role in the Boston rebellion two years later.

All the soundings of the Bell noted above are drawn from remaining official records. It must be considered, however, that the pealing of the Bell was not merely confined to political affairs; it was also pressed into service by religious and secular organizations which had no other means of summoning their members. A major fire could activate the Bell, as could the death of a prominent citizen. The record does not show how many times in the course of a day — or week — the Bell tolled. Its clang was loud; a necessity in order to summon those who lived at remote distances from the State House. The area around the State House, however, was largely residential and the pealing gradually became a severe annoyance to those in the immediate vicinity, implying a much heavier use of the Bell than has been put in the record.

On September 16, 1772, a petition was drawn and read to the Assembly by a group of distraught citizens in an effort to curtail the noise. It said, in part:

. . . from divers inhabitants of the City of Philadelphia, living near the State House . . . setting forth, that they are much incommoded and distressed by the too frequent Ringing by the great Bell in the Steeple of the State House, the inconvenience of which has often been felt severely when some of the Petitioners' families have been affected with sickness, at which times, from its uncommon size and unusual sound, it is extremely dangerous and may prove fatal; — that the Petitioners conceive that it was never designed to be rung on any other than public Occasions, such as the Times of Meeting of the Honourable Assembly of the Province, and of the Courts of Justice; — that the Petitioners, therefore, intreat the House to interpose and relieve them from this great and dangerous inconvenience so far as to prevent the ringing of said great Bell on any other than public occasions."

Thus spoke a segment of Philadelphia, presumably with ears constantly buzzing from the unceasing ringing of the Bell, who were kind enough to avoid describing it as "too loud," but rather said it had an "unusual sound." The petition was ordered "laid upon the table for further consideration" and there is no record of any reply to it. The petition accomplished one thing, however; it spurred some to think that perhaps the vibrations from the ringing might have a damaging effect on the steeple itself. A year later, the Assembly called for "some skillful carpenter to report on the present state of the steeple."

By 1773, the issue of tea tax had become a fiery one and a lively symbol of the impending Revolution. On October 18, the Bell called a Town Meeting together to pass resolutions against buyers and vendors of tea, both groups being labelled "enemies of the country." On the day of the meeting, however, the ship *Polly* was en route from England with a bulging cargo of tea destined for Philadelphia. News of the landing of the vessel — and of its undesirable cargo — burst forth on December 27 and the Bell was hurriedly pressed into service to summon another Town Meeting.

Resolutions forbidding the *Polly* to land its cargo were immediately adopted and passed. A march to the loading dock by the crowd followed and, to the astonishment of the *Polly's* captain, he was ordered to sail back to England, leaving no record of his visit. Evidently the gentleman was well versed in evaluating the mood of a crowd; after provisioning his vessel for the return trip, one historian notes that ". . . the tea vessel, the captain and the tea sailed down the river to return no more."

The famous Boston Tea Party took place on December 16, 1773, and throughout the following year additional hostile acts occurred toward ships bearing tea. The Boston disorders, however, infuriated the British and on June 1, 1774, they closed the port. The Bell was muffled and tolled to bring the word to Philadelphians. Seventeen days later, the Bell again tolled to call a meeting subscribing funds for Bostonians suffering from the effects of the blockade. The general citizenry raised £2,000 and the Friends of Philadelphia Meeting subscribed £2,450 in gold, all of which was duly sent to Boston.

The succession of incidents which had begun as varying acts of rebellion on the part of the Americans had now become outright defiance and resultant reprisals by the English brought an irreparable polarization between Britain and her trans-Atlantic Colonies. The closing of Boston's port and a number of other restrictions summed up as the "Intolerable Acts" further limited the civil liberties of the colonists and by June of 1774, Samuel Adams urged the formation and meeting of a Continental Congress to "agree on effectual measures for defeating the despotic designs of those who were endeavoring to effect the ruin of the colonies." He suggested a September meeting of such a body and so it was that on September 5, 1774, the First Continental Congress met at Carpenter's Hall in Philadelphia. No recorded sounding of the Bell exists for that date; it's entirely possible that such a ringing may even have been forbidden. The delegates were bound to an oath of secrecy and all meetings were held behind closed doors.

Enmity between British and Americans heightened with each passing day and English determination to punish the colonists for their defiance intensified. In February of 1775, a Restraining Act was introduced, designed to prevent the New England Colonies from trading with any nation other than Great Britain (and the British West Indies), and barring New Englanders from fishing the North Atlantic. The act was then amended to include New Jersey, Pennsylvania, Maryland, Virginia and South Carolina. Patrick Henry, the volatile insurgent from Virginia stepped to the fore again with his famous "Liberty or Death" speech to the House of Burgesses, and General Gage, leading the British troops in Boston, received orders from England to strike the Colonies at once — even if it meant war.

The mounting turmoil erupted in the Battle of Lexington on April 19, 1775, and on April 25, the Bell performed the unhappy mission of summoning Philadelphians to hear the news. The State House yard was filled with grim-faced colonists as they learned the outcome of the battle and the magnitude of American casualties.

Nearly eight thousand people gathered in the yard that day and their mood can be seen sharply in the resolution they passed unanimously "to associate, for the purpose of defending with arms, their lives, liberty and property against all attempts to deprive them of them."

Now the stage was set.

Free
and
Independent States

THERE IS ALWAYS SOME FACTOR OF MYTH, LEGEND OR JUST plain confusion present in the history of any country. Historians have a way of disagreeing with each other in interpreting existing knowledge differently or, in some cases, misunderstanding events which were recorded many years in the past. Add to this the intrusion of the romanticists, particularly writers who would fictionalize history and thus create new myths and legends — and some idea of the errors possible in reporting historical events may be gained.

The Liberty Bell was no exception. For a national symbol which grew, in effect, into a world-wide symbol of freedom, it has had a wealth of misinformation disseminated about it. Other myths have surrounded the actual date on which we declared our independence, as well as the document that our Colonial legislators considered the one which severed ties with Britain.

But the Bell was unaware of the myths and legends it would engender and at the outset of the Revolution continued performing its designed functions faithfully. Philadelphia of 1775 was a busier city than it had ever been. The Battle of Lexington had triggered everyone into action and conversation was almost exclusively directed toward the war. Division among the people was more apparent than ever before; the rebels openly proclaimed their defiance of England while the conservative and loyalist Tories maintained more discreet silences and hoped everything would come out all right. In between were the Quakers who, as pacifists, were not held in high esteem by the rebels, as would be demonstrated many times over during the course of the war.

Less than a month after Lexington, the Bell announced the convening of the Second Continental Congress in the State House and the legislators hurriedly began making preparations for the coming conflict. One of the delegates from Virginia was a tall, handsome man who bore himself with an astonishing dignity. He rarely smiled and showed no inclination toward camaraderie with other members of the Assembly. He had made a modest reputation as a military man and shortly after the Congress began its session, there was talk that he might be asked to serve as Commander-in-Chief of the Continental Forces. After much debate and discussion, he ultimately accepted, although not without denying that he had the talent for such an assignment, and the fledgling nation had its first military leader — George Washington.

He departed from Philadelphia almost immediately to begin preparations for assuming his new command. Our loosely strung forces were already facing the British in several areas, nearly all of the skirmishes ending in disaster for the American rebels. Most notable of these encounters was the Battle of Bunker Hill which the British won, but at a high cost in casualties. Washington had not yet made his presence felt by the Continental Army and did not actually assume command until July 3, 1775, two weeks after Bunker Hill.

In October of 1775, Congress authorized formation of a "Navy," a pitiful marine force which consisted of four ships at its inception. In all, the future did not promise well for the rebels, but the balance sheet was not entirely one-sided. The Americans were fighting on familiar ground while the British were far from home with an enormously long supply line to keep in operation. One telling advantage held by the Americans was the superiority of their rifles over the smoothbore British musket, both in range and accuracy. However, the shortage of both arms and ammunition which plagued the Americans did little to help the superiority of the weapon. And they were largely untrained men, rendering them less effective as a military team.

While the British enjoyed many more advantages in the military sense, they also suffered from three major disadvantages which probably contributed in large part to their ultimate defeat. First, they would not or could not adapt to the highly unconventional "guerilla" or frontier-style warfare employed by the Americans. Second, they failed to conscript a Loyalist army for peripheral support. And third, they held the Americans in contempt, a condition which led them constantly to underestimate Washington and his raggle-taggle army.

1776 started off with a loud bang from Tom Paine who published his now-famous "Common Sense" in January. In it, he flayed George III and the monarchical form of government with such force and simplicity that many "fence-sitters" or outright opponents of the rebels were won over to the Revolutionary side.

Two bright spots appeared suddenly in the spring of '76, by which

Richard Henry Lee's Resolution, believed to be in Lee's handwriting. *Library of Congress.*

time the Revolution was in full swing. In March, the British decided to evacuate Boston and, in that same month, the reigning monarchs in France and Spain elected to extend aid to the colonists. With monies advanced by both countries, the Continental Army received more than 80% of their necessary military supplies during 1776-77.

While there was no question that a full-scale war was in progress, there had yet to be any formal declaration of war or statement of intent to gain independence out of Philadelphia. And none came until June 7, 1776, when Virginia delegate Richard Henry Lee offered a resolution which began: "These United Colonies are, and of right ought to be, free and independent States; that they are absolved from all allegiance to the British Crown and that all political connection between them and the State of Great Britain, is and ought to be totally absolved. . . ."

The resolution was received with enthusiasm by the Congress but a vote was postponed pending action on a plan for confederation. Finally, on July 2, Lee's resolution was voted on and passed, and it was this document that was generally considered to be the deciding factor in the ultimate break with Great Britain. But even while the Lee resolution was being proposed, a formal Declaration of Independence was in the making. The Congress had drafted a committee consisting of Thomas Jefferson, Ben Franklin, John Adams, Robert R. Livingston and Roger Sherman to prepare it. And so it was already in discussion and the committee had decided that Jefferson should be its author. This move had been designed as a safeguard in the event the Lee resolution failed to pass.

So pleased was John Adams at the passage of the Lee resolution that he wrote to his wife the following day, July 3:

Yesterday the greatest question was decided, which was ever debated in America; and a greater perhaps, never was nor will be decided among men. A resolution was passed, without one dissenting colony, 'that these United Colonies are, and of right ought to be, free and independent. . . . You will see in a few days a declaration setting forth the causes which have impelled us to this mighty resolution and the reasons which will justify it in the sight of God and man.

Thomas Jefferson painted by Charles Wilson Peale in 1791. *National Park Service.*

Richard Henry Lee painted by Charles Wilson Peale in 1784. *National Park Service.*

A few hours later on that same day Adams, enthusiasm still at a peak, was prompted to send a second letter:

The Second day of July, 1776, will be the most memorable epoch in the history of America. I am apt to believe it will be celebrated by succeeding generations as the great anniversary festival. . . . It ought to be solemnized with pomp and parade, with shows, games, sports, guns, bells, bonfires and illuminations, from one end of this continent to the other, from this time forward, forevermore.

Despite Adams' hearty proposal of the Second of July as our national holiday, the Lee resolution became all but lost to American history; it was the eloquent and more sophisticated document written by Thomas Jefferson, the Declaration of Independence, that captured the fierce passion and spirit of the Revolution and spurred the imagination of every rebel in the Colonies. When, on July 4, 1776, Jefferson's version of the Declaration as amended by Congress was unanimously adopted, the birth of an independent republic became an accomplished fact. Now it was up to the old State House Bell to "Proclaim Liberty throughout all the land and to all the inhabitants thereof" — in short, to sound off for independence and it did just that — but not on July 4.

Oddly enough, although the Declaration was approved by all present on July 4, only the name of John Hancock, as President of the Second Continental Congress, was affixed to the document. Years later, Jefferson was to insist that all members of the Congress signed that day. However, intensive research has shown that the famous signatures were placed on a copy which had been engrossed on July 19 and actually signed by most of the delegates on August 2. Even then, not all signatures were placed on this copy, and the last man to sign, Thomas McKean of Delaware, did so early in 1777.

Thus, although the Declaration was adopted on July 4, it was neither signed nor publicly proclaimed on that day. The Fourth of July fell on a Thursday and the Jefferson document passed late in the day. The original manuscript was sent to a printer and copies were produced during the night and placed in the hands of the designated parties on the fifth. John Hancock sent a copy to General

Washington, suggesting that he proclaim it at the head of the Army "in the way you shall think most proper."

A number of letters were now prepared to be sent to individuals concerned, and each letter contained a copy of the Declaration. The first of these letters was probably sent to the Pennsylvania Committee of Safety with a request that the committee "suggest the propriety of proclaiming it in such a mode that the people may be universally informed of it." The committee's job now was to set a time for a public reading of the document. At a meeting called on July 6, it was decided that the following Monday, July 8, be designated as the day of proclamation. Letters were then sent to Bucks, Chester, Northampton, Lancaster and Berks counties, asking that each county proclaim the Declaration on that date also.

More specifically, the plans decided upon by the Committee read as follows:

> ORDERED, That the Sheriff of Philadelphia read, and cause to be proclaimed at the State House, in the City of Philadelphia, on Monday, the eighth day of July, instant, at 12 o'clock, at noon, of the same day, the Declaration of the United Colonies of America, and that he cause all his Officers and the Constables of the said City, to attend the reading thereof.
>
> RESOLVED, That every member of this Committee, in or near the City, be ordered to meet at the Committee Chamber, before 12 o'clock, on Monday, to proceed to the State House, where the Declaration of Independence is to be proclaimed.

All of which leaves no doubt concerning the actual date of the public proclamation of the Declaration. The Committee of Inspection of the City and Liberties was requested to attend also, and one of the members, Christopher Marshall, noted in his diary as of July 6:

> Near eight, went to Committee, Philosophical Hall. Agreed the Declaration be declared at the State House, next second day. At same time, the King's Arms there are to be taken down by Nine Associators, here appointed, who are to convey it to a pile of casks erected upon the Commons, for the purpose of a bonfire, and the arms placed

upon the top. This being election day, I opposed the motion, only by having this put off till next day, fearing it would interrupt the election, but the motion was carried by a majority.

The Committee had done its work well and now the city was ready for a public declaration. The parts of the drama leading up to it had been enacted behind closed doors but, by the weekend of July 6-7, the word was out — broadside copies of the Declaration were being distributed and the full text appeared in the July 6 issue of *The Pennsylvania Packet.* But the Bell waited.

July 8, 1776, according to Christopher Marshall's diary, dawned as a "warm sunshine morning." Since word of the adoption of the Declaration and the time of its proclamation had leaked out via coffee house channels and other avenues, it is conceivable that the crowd began to assemble in the State House yard long before noon. Marshall himself started for the yard at eleven o'clock, in company with the Committee of Inspection.

At some point between eleven and twelve o'clock, the Old One and all the other city bells began to ring to summon the populace. Their peals could only be joyous ones — this would climax the greatest week in American history. Shortly before twelve, a tall, portly

John Nixon, who read the Declaration of Independence at the State House on July 8, 1776. *Historical Society of Pennsylvania.*

gentleman clutching a copy of the Declaration slowly ascended the steps to a platform in the State House yard. This gentleman, Colonel John Nixon, had been asked by the city sheriff to read the document and, at precisely twelve o'clock, he did. The bells ceased during the reading and, when Colonel Nixon was finished, they once more pealed out their joyous sounds for all the world to hear. Three loud huzzahs swelled up at the conclusion of the reading and the entire city turned to celebrating throughout the rest of the day and into the night. According to Marshall, "There were bonfires, ringing bells, with other great demonstrations of joy upon the unanimity and agreement of the Declaration."

Today we have the unmistaken identity of the man who read the contents of the Declaration to the people of Philadelphia. Colonel John Nixon was the son of one Richard Nixon, an early Irish immigrant who settled in Westchester, Pennsylvania, where his son John was born. John, who became a Philadelphia merchant and an ardent Patriot, was chosen as a member of the Committee of Safety on its founding and was for a time its president. He was also one of the founders of The Friendly Sons of St. Patrick, formed in 1771. He commanded the Third Philadelphia Battalion during the Revolution and spent that terrible winter at Valley Forge with Washington. While he was there, the British burned his country home. After the war, he became a bank president and remained so until his death in 1809.

With the election of Richard M. Nixon to the Presidency of the United States, there has been an inclination to consider him a direct descendant of Colonel John Nixon, whose father's name was Richard. Unfortunately, this is not so. Our thirty-seventh President is descended from Revolutionary stock on both sides, but his paternal ancestor was James Nixon, who settled in Brandywine Hundred, New Castle County, Delaware, in 1731. James came from Northern Ireland and his occupation lists him first as a cooper, then a farmer and finally as a yeoman, or landowner. He had two sons and four daughters and it is from son George, who distinguished himself in the battles of Brandywine and Princeton during the Revolution, that Richard Milhous Nixon is descended.

The Fall
of
Philadelphia

HOW OFTEN THE BELL RANG DURING THE YEAR FOLLOWING the Declaration of Independence is not known, but from its lofty tower above Chestnut Street it looked down upon a transformed city. More military personnel now appeared on the streets, some en route to their battalions, some in town on leaves. Since enlistments were of short duration, there were presumably many who had also had enough of the war and were making their way back to their homes. It was often difficult to distinguish a soldier from a civilian unless he was carrying a rifle and a pack. Many of our soldiers had no uniforms and wore their everyday work clothes into battle.

The unfortunate soldiers stationed at Valley Forge with Washington not only lacked uniforms, many of them had no shoes or any kind of adequate outer clothing to protect them from that abominable winter of constant snow and freezing temperatures. In Philadelphia, less than twenty-five miles away, the civilians hurried about their business a bit faster than before and the expressions on their faces were grim and concerned. New and alien faces and costumes appeared as a result of Congress' drive to recruit foreign officers for the Army as advisers and experts in various fields. The first call for such men — put out by Silas Deane — resulted in an enormous influx of military men from many countries, all milling about Philadelphia and all claiming commissions in the embryo Army. The confusion was mighty and screening almost impossible. Congress, in desperation, ordered that in the future any foreign military personnel sent to Philadelphia must bear valid qualifications and demonstrate proven ability in their fields.

The foreign recruitment campaign was successful, however. It gave us the Marquis de Lafayette, Baron Johann de Kalb, Thaddeus Kosciusko and Baron von Steuben, all men who served our forces wisely and well.

The war itself was not going well, although bright spots here and there showed that it was far from being a lost cause. The August, 1776, Battle of Long Island found the British the victors and the Americans sent into full retreat at a frightful casualty count. In September, the British occupied Manhattan and captured Nathan Hale, who was hanged as a spy almost immediately. The Battle of White Plains was another disaster for the Americans, but the end of the year witnessed Washington's victory at Trenton, followed by victory at Princeton in January of 1777. The ledger sheet was somewhat in balance, but not evenly. In May of '77, Congress authorized a new banner — The Stars and Stripes — and now, for the first time, a single flag could fly above our fighting forces.

As July approached, Philadelphia seethed with a new excitement: the first anniversary of independence was at hand. In spite of military defeats and the knowledge that General Howe was planning to invade and occupy the city, Philadelphia was determined to celebrate. Again the Bell waited, ready to peal out widely when the festivities began. That they were a success is seen in this account which appeared in *The Pennsylvania Gazette* on July 9, 1777:

> Friday, the 4th of July inst. being the Anniversary of the Independence of the United States of America, was celebrated in this city with demonstrations of joy and festivity. About noon all the armed ships and galleys in the river were drawn up before the city, dressed

in the gayest manner, with the colours of the United States and streamers displayed. At one o'clock, the yards being properly manned, they began the celebration of the day by a discharge of thirteen cannon from each of the ships, and one from each of the thirteen galleys, in honour of the thirteen United States. In the afternoon an elegant dinner was prepared for Congress. . . . After dinner a number of toasts were drank, all breathing independence, and a generous love of liberty, and commemorating the memories of those brave and worthy patriots who gallantly exposed their lives, and fell gloriously in defense of freedom, and the righteous cause of their country. . . . Towards evening, several troops of horse, a corps of artillery, and a brigade of North Carolina forces, which was in town on its way to join the grand army, were drawn up in Second Street and received by Congress and the General Officers. The evening was closed with the ringing of bells, and at night there was a grand exhibition of fireworks (which began and concluded with thirteen rockets) on the commons, and the city was beautifully illuminated. Everything was conducted with the greatest order and decorum, and the face of joy and gladness was universal

There's no doubt about it; the first birthday party was a huge success, even though the ringing of the Great Bell is perfunctorily included with all bells in the newspaper accounts. Inveterate letter-writer John Adams, writing to his twelve-year-old daughter on July 5, elaborates a bit further on the occasion:

MY DEAR DAUGHTER:
Yesterday, being the Anniversary of American independence, was celebrated here with a festivity and ceremony becoming the occasion. I am too old to delight in pretty descriptions, if I had a talent for them, otherwise a picture might be drawn which would please the fancy of a Whig at least.

Following the opening, he describes essentially the same things that appeared in the *Gazette* account but concludes with another reference to the bells:

In the evening I was walking about the streets for a little fresh aire

In Council of Safety.

Philadelphia, December 2, 1776.

RESOLVED,

THAT it is the Opinion of this Board, that all the Shops in this City be fhut up, that the Schools be broke up, and the Inhabitants engaged folely in providing for the Defence of this City, at this Time of extreme Danger.

By Order of Council,
DAVID RITTENHOUSE, Vice-Prefident.

[Philadelphia, Printed by Henry Miller, in Race-ftreet.]

By ORDER of His EXCELLENCY

Sir William Howe, K. B.

General and Commander in Chief, &c. &c. &c.

PROCLAMATION.

I DO hereby give Notice to the Inhabitants of the City of Philadelphia and its Environs, it is the Order of His Excellency, that " No Perfon whatever, living " within the faid City and its Environs, fhall appear in " the Streets between the Beating of the Tattoo, at Half " an Hour after Eight o'Clock in the Evening, and the " Revellie in the Morning, without Lanthorns: And all " who fhall be found abroad, within the Time aforefaid, " will be liable to be examined by the Patroles, and con- " fined, unlefs they fhall give a fatisfactory Account of " themfelves." And I do hereby enjoin and require the Inhabitants, and all others refiding in the faid City and its Environs, to pay ftrict Obedience to the faid Order, and govern themfelves accordingly.

Given under my Hand at Philadelphia, this 9th Day of January, in the Eighteenth Year of His Majefty's Reign.   JOS. GALLOWAY,

Superintendent-General.

and exercise, and was surprised to find the whole city lighting up their candles at their windows. I walked most of the evening, and I think it was the most splendid illumination I ever saw; a few surly houses were dark, but the lights were very universal. Considering the lateness of the design, and the suddenness of the execution, I was amazed at the universal joy and alacrity that was discovered, and the brilliancy and splendour of every part of this joyful exhibition. I had forgot the ringing of bells all day and evening, and the bonfires in the streets, and the fireworks played off.

Had General Howe been here in disguise, or his master, this show would have given them the heartache. I am your affectionate father,

JOHN ADAMS

"The ringing of bells all day and evening" must certainly have transformed the sounds of the city on that happy birthday into something resembling a foundry working a twenty-four-hour shift. But what a joyous sound to the Patriots who had achieved a whole year of independence! And what a bane to those who drew up the petition against the Bell in 1772! In any case, the Great Bell took an active, happy part in the country's first birthday.

In spite of the glowing accounts of love and affection expressed by the *Gazette* and John Adams, however, there is more than a little suspicion that things may have gotten a bit out of hand during the celebration. Adams himself hinted at one of the causes when he told his daughter that "a few surly houses were dark." These houses were probably those of Quakers who would not take part in a celebration predicated on war. The Friends were constant targets of the more irrational Patriots and penalties were obviously paid that birthday night by those whose windows displayed no birthday candles. Prolific diarist Elizabeth Drinker, herself a Quaker, notes in her journal for the day that "The Town illuminated and a great number of windows broken on ye Anniversary of Independence and Freedom."

But the headiness of celebration faded quickly with the realization that the suspected attack on Philadelphia might be coming soon. The British had been highly frustrated for a year; despite their victories, they had not been able to rout the Continental Army and now

The Cadwallader house, Philadelphia, was used by Howe as his head-quarters during the occupation. From Bryant's *Popular History of the United States.*

it seemed that more stringent measures were needed. A plan for a massive three-pronged attack on the various American Armies was approved and to it, General Howe added a plan for a sea attack on Philadelphia. It, too, was approved. This may have been another example of British underestimation and failure to understand the complexities of these contemptible Colonials. The reasoning may have been that if Philadelphia could be taken, Patriot morale would be broken and the war brought to a quick end.

While it was true that Philadelphia was the capital of this brash new republic, it was not a London or a Paris, nor had it acquired the host of national and executive functions attached to any European capital. More than that, its government was fluid and mobile. When the British did arrive, the Congress quickly moved to Lancaster, and later to York, and continued to function with almost no loss of time or effort. But the British were determined to take the key Colonial city and, after thrashing the Americans at Brandywine and Paoli, General Howe led his victorious army into Penn's Greene Country Towne on September 26, 1777.

One important area of underestimation by the British was the effectiveness of American espionage. Howe's plans were well known to Congress and the American military much in advance of his arrival. And so, with little fanfare, everything that might be of value to the English was spirited away and all movable supplies quickly sent into hiding.

"Movable supplies" included all the city's bells, a juicy prize for any invading army of the day. Bells contained metal that could be melted down and made into musket shot and cannon balls. A victorious army, short of supplies, would head for the steeples of a conquered town, remove the bells and melt them down. There is evidence that the city fathers were unhanging all the city's bells as much as two weeks before Howe's arrival. In her journal for September 15, Elizabeth Drinker notes: "I have heard from two or three persons today that ye church bells are being taken down; ye bridge over the Schuylkill taken up and ye Ropes across ye Ferry cut."

A week later Miss Drinker made the following entry, with some finality:

> . . . all ye bells in ye city are certainly taken away and there is also talk of Pump Handles and Fire Buckets being taken also, but that may be only conjecture. Things seem to be, upon ye whole drawing towards great confusion. May we be strengthened in the time of trial.

It is reasonably safe to assume that the British were angered when they realized that the city's bells had been spirited away, and especially at the loss of the State House Bell. It was one of the biggest in Philadelphia, its only rival being the largest of the Christ Church ring, and would have been an excellent source of musket shot. If there is any doubt as to the value of such a bell through its conversion to shot, some simple arithmetic clears that immediately.

The average British musket ball approached an ounce in weight. (The American rifle ball weighed about a half-ounce, but its deadlier accuracy more than made up for its lesser weight.) The Bell weighed 2,080 pounds. At sixteen one-ounce musket balls to the pound, the Bell would have given the British about thirty-three thousand rounds of ammunition, allowing for some losses in the conversion. That would be enough to kill quite a few Americans. And that was the yield from only one bell, which explains why all of the bells had to go.

And so the British, led by General Howe, marched into Philadelphia on a warm September afternoon, only to find it somewhat meaningless. Everything that might have been of value to them had vanished. They came in anyway, relatively quietly for a victorious army. A Quaker lady wrote in her diary for September 26: "Well, here are the English in earnest. About 3,000 came in through Second Street without opposition or interruption."

But there was no Bell in the State House to ring them in.

Northampton
Town

E VACUATION OF THE CITY'S BELLS WAS A MAJOR ENGINEERING
project. And, when the order for removal was officially
issued by the Supreme Executive Council of Pennsylvania
on September 14, 1777, the removers had to act with lightning speed
in spite of one gargantuan handicap; they had to work largely under
cover of darkness.

The order to remove the bells was passed along to Colonel Benjamin Flower, Commissary General of Military Stores, and his instructions read:

> ORDERED: that Colonel Flower employ James Worrell, Francis Allison
> and Mr. Evans, Carpenters, or such other workmen as he may think
> proper to employ, to take down the Bells of all the public Buildings in
> this city and convey them to safety.

They had their work cut out for them. Colonel Flower was charged
not only with getting the bells down, but also conveying them to
safety. Eleven bells in all had to be removed and, according to his-

torian John Baer Stoudt, an authority on the Bell and its history, their combined weight was probably about twelve thousand pounds. Most had to be taken from fairly high steeples, loaded aboard wagons and spirited from the city.

The bells could be lowered through a system of trap doors in the church steeples and the State House tower without calling attention to the stealthy plan, but taking them from the buildings had to be done in the dark of night. Philadelphia was crawling with Tories and probably with British spies working in advance of Howe's oncoming legions, but so far as is known, word of the bells' unhanging and flight did not reach the General until it was too late to overtake them.

Once the bells had been grounded and temporarily secreted, Colonel Flower's next assignment was to convey them to safety. Since Flower was an Army man, and Army transport wagons bearing valuable government documents and materials were leaving the area with increasing frequency, he might naturally lean toward the military to provide transport for his precious cargo. On the other hand, should the bells be put into the military vehicles and be overtaken by the British, they would certainly end up as shot designed for Americans.

His reasoning then might have led him to seek out farmers bringing produce into the city from the area where the bells were destined to go — Allentown (then Northampton Town). Traditionally, these Pennsylvania German farmers brought their wares into Philadelphia and returned to their farms north of the city with empty wagons. A few of these wagons, with the bells secreted in them and covered with hay or straw, might be a better device. Should the British pass such a convoy, there would be a slightly lesser chance that they would be searched.

If that were the case, and the only real evidence today seems to favor the farm-wagon method, then Flower would have to find a number of friendly, close-mouthed Pennsylvania German farmers to cooperate.

Legend has it today that he did, and the man who was chosen to cart the Bell was one John Jacob Mickley. The identity of the other bell carriers is unknown. Concomitant with finding trustworthy drivers, Flower also had to find places of refuge for the bells once they reached Allentown. We know today from documentary evidence that he succeeded in his mission.

The exact date of the bells' departure is unknown, a tribute, perhaps, to the extent of Flower's well-kept secret. Some historians give the date of September 16 or 17 for the completion of the unhangings; Elizabeth Drinker's diary speculates that all bells had been removed from Philadelphia by September 23. Whatever the exact day, Howe marched into Philadelphia on September 27 but did not send a patrol in pursuit of the fleeing wagon train, undoubtedly because of the need for men to secure the city and repulse Washington's counterattack at Germantown on October 4. Very much aware, however, that the citizens of Philadelphia had hidden or removed as much useable material as possible, Howe issued the following proclamation on September 29:

> All persons having in their possession any kind of stores and provisions belonging to the Rebel Army are hereby required to report the same to the Quarter-Master or Commissary General. . . . "

But by then the Bell was on its way north, out of reach whether or not it was reported.

Two conjectures on the route taken by the Bell are open. It may have gone directly to Bethlehem and from there to Allentown or, second, it may have been taken along the river toward Trenton and thence to Bethlehem cross-country. There is some plausability in the Trenton route. Rumors had been spread that the bells were sunk in the Delaware River and the wagons may have been given this route to corroborate the rumors and thus discourage the British from instituting a search for them.

At some point along the rugged route, the bell wagons joined an Army convoy of some seven hundred other wagons. This meeting probably took place along the Bethlehem Pike near Montgomeryville, but whether the meeting was planned or merely accidental is not recorded. Now the bell wagons were given the further anonymity of being part of a huge train and presumably the drivers felt better about it. The train they had joined contained, in large part, refugees and their personal possessions, along with wagons bearing other valuable "stores and provisions."

In a manner much below its dignity, the Great Bell — hidden from view by an ample covering of stable refuse — rattled and bumped along the rutted, muddy road to Bethlehem. It was to endure the journey in this odd caravan for many days and suffer even more indignity when its great weight finally broke the wagon just as the train reached the center of Bethlehem.

The diary of the Moravian congregation in Bethlehem gives us an exact time of arrival for the Bell in that city. The day is noted as September 24, some eight to ten days after its exit from Philadelphia depending on the departure date. The diary states under its entry for the above date:

> The whole of the heavy baggage of the army, in a continuous train of 700 wagons, direct from camp, arrived under escort of 200 men, commanded by Colonel [William] Polk of North Carolina. They encamped on the south side of the Lehigh [river] and in one night destroyed all our buckwheat and the fences around the fields. The wagons, after unloading, return to Trenton for more stores. Among the things brought here were the church bells from Philadelphia and

the wagon in which was loaded the State House bell, broke down in the street and had to be unloaded.

The account makes no mention of whether the Bell tumbled out of the wagon, or merely squashed the wagon with its weight. The sight of seven hundred wagons coming into such a small town must surely have been a thing of awe — and bitter resentment — to the citizens of Bethlehem. The small town (by 1780, Bethlehem consisted of thirty-six houses occupied by sixty-one families) had already been overrun by the American Army and turned into a military hospital. Homes and public buildings had been appropriated for quartering and the moans and muffled cries of the sick and wounded were heard continuously. Soldiers and officers were everywhere and the atmosphere consisted largely of confusion, frenzy and chaos. The entire town was in trauma, but the ordeal was not

"The First Journey of the Liberty Bell" painted by Edwin Willard Deming, circa 1900. The original of this famous painting disappeared in the 1930's and is being sought by Independence Hall National Historical Park for display. *National Park Service.*

over. Before that week was ended, two hundred wagons arrived with more refugees and wounded. Whether or not the good burghers of Bethlehem lent a hand to get the Bell out of the damaged wagon and into another is not known; if they didn't, they are not to be censured.

The unfortunate breakdown of the wagon and subsequent disenfranchisement of the Bell occurred, according to historian Victor Rosewater, "somewhere in towards the descent to the mill, in the large, open space in front of the Brethren's House, then spoken of as 'der Platz' or the Square."

The breakdown surely caused more than a little concern and once again it would seem that speed in effecting the transfer was of the essence. No matter how the situation was handled, the Bell would be exposed . . . and who knew whether a Howe informant might be lurking in the curious crowd that gathered about the wagon? Accordingly, the transfer was made to a wagon owned and driven by Frederick Leaser, who thereupon carted the Bell to Allentown.

The Bell's hiding place until 1778 was in the basement of the Zion High German Reformed Church of Allentown, where it arrived early on the morning of September 25. Other bells were hidden in the same basement and the Church above them served as a military hospital until the British evacuated Philadelphia.

John Jacob Mickley and Frederick Leaser both have commemorative tablets in Pennsylvania which honor the parts they played in the saving of the Bell. The Leaser tablet stands on Route 143 between Jacksonville and Wanamaker near Leaser Lake in the upper western corner of Lehigh County. The tablet dedicated to Mickley is now outside the entrance to the Liberty Bell Shrine in Allentown. The shrine was dedicated in 1962 and is housed in the same basement where the Bell was harbored during its year-long stay in Allentown. The tablet reads:

In commemoration of the saving of the Liberty Bell from the British in September, 1777. Erected to the memory of John Jacob Mickley, Commissionary of Issues and member of the General Committee from Whitehall Township, Northampton County, Pennsylvania, who, under cover of darkness, and with his farm team hauled the Liberty Bell from Independence Hall, Philadelphia, through the British lines to

Bethlehem. When the wagon broke down, September 22, 1777, the Bell was then transferred to Frederick Leiser's [*sic*] wagon and brought to Allentown, September 24, 1777. It was placed beneath the floor of Zion's Reformed Church where it remained secreted for nearly a year.

The Liberty Bell Shrine now contains a full-scale replica of the Old One. It is one of fifty-three bells cast in 1950 to promote a federal Savings Bond drive and was given to the shrine by the Pennsylvania Historical and Museum Commission who had received it from the federal government through Treasury Secretary John F. Snyder. This replica is a happy reminder of a day when the Great Bell needed shelter, and found it among the good people of Allentown. It also evokes the image of the Reverend Abraham Blumer, pastor of Zion Church in 1777. The Reverend Blumer, anxious to provide haven for this sacred relic, stripped off his coat and enthusiastically joined in the lowering of the Bell into the church's cellar.

When the British completed their evacuation of Philadelphia on June 18, 1777, the bells at Allentown were free to leave their dark places of refuge and lost no time in doing so. It is recorded that they departed on June 27 and on August 22, the *Pennsylvania Packet* stated that "The bells of this City . . . are all returned safe and hung again." Where they had been between those dates is unknown.

Four years later, however, the peace of the Old One was again disturbed when the steeple, deteriorating and in danger of toppling, was removed. The Bell was unhung, lowered to a level within the brick portion of the tower and roofed over. Now, instead of sounding from the open heights of the steeple, it was enclosed by louvres. In 1781, thirty years after its initial ordering by Norris, the Bell's pealing could no longer reach the distant boundaries of Philadelphia; there was still life in the Bell, but it had passed its prime.

The Late Years
of
the Old One

A LTHOUGH THE BELL WAS BACK IN PLACE BY MID-1778, THE war continued as an armed conflict until 1781 and it was 1783 before final peace terms were agreed upon. The years between 1778 and 1781 were maddening, frustrating years with the tide of battle switching capriciously from one side to the other with no recognizable pattern. The British, now under the command of General Henry Clinton, left Philadelphia for New York, although not without suffering a stinging defeat at the hands of the Americans en route at the Battle of Monmouth Court House, New Jersey, which began the evening of June 27, 1778.

The streets of Philadelphia were more crowded than ever with people of all nationalities moving in and out, individuals on government business of one sort or another scurrying about, soldiers coming and going and the general citizenry, caught up in the tensions of war, looking just a bit more grim than they had in the early years of the struggle.

The British were scoring victories in the South, but the Americans were doing a bit better in the North. Spain joined France on the

American side, and the pitifully inadequate American Navy was doing its best to demonstrate strength, as it did in a surprising victory by John Paul Jones, sailing the *Bonhomme Richard* into battle with the English.

But in 1780 the ugly spectre of mutiny arose when Connecticut regiments rebelled at Morristown and had to be held in check by Pennsylvania troops. Benedict Arnold insured his place in history as a traitor and, as the war drew to a close in 1781, Pennsylvania troops staged a mutiny in New Jersey. Like the Connecticut mutiny, however, it was short-lived. Viewing these mutinous acts objectively, it is truly surprising that more of the same was not manifest. Considering the lack of food, clothing and arms and ammunition, it is almost astonishing that our troops held together as well as they did, and that they clung tenaciously to the determination to bring the war to a victorious conclusion.

Which is what they did at Yorktown. By October 2, 1781, Cornwallis had been battered into submission at that tiny Virginia town and his dismal counterattack had failed to even the score. Cornwallis attempted to escape across the York River but a sudden storm forced him to abandon his plan. On the 17th, he indicated a desire to open negotiations for surrender and the capitulation of the British Army became official on the 18th. The next day nearly eight thousand British troops laid down their arms. Their actual surrender and casualty list at Yorktown added up to the following:

> Surrendered: 7,527 troops
> 840 seamen
> Killed : 156
> Wounded : 326
> Missing : 70

The Americans lost 23 dead, 65 wounded and 30 missing. The French, who were present in great numbers, suffered 60 dead and 193 wounded.

There is a note of bitter irony seen in Cornwallis' surrender. On the day he showed the white flag, British General Clinton sailed from New York with massive re-enforcements of seven thousand troops and thirty-five ships. Had Cornwallis endured his siege and held out for ten more days, the war might have taken on an entirely different flavor. When Clinton heard of the surrender, he turned back and Yorktown remained the site of the unofficial end of the War of Independence, although a formal treaty was not signed until 1783.

How many times — and for what reasons — the Great Bell was rung between its return to Philadelphia and the Battle of Yorktown will never be known. But there is no question that it rang out wildly when the news from Yorktown reached Philadelphia.

On the day of Cornwallis' submission, Washington was concerned with an inordinate amount of detail related to the victory and it wasn't until late at night that he finally drafted a letter to Philadelphia describing the events of the day. There are two versions of how and when the Bell was rung on receipt of the news. According to Lossing's *Pictorial Field Book,* General Washington sent Lieutenant Colonel Tench Tilghman, a Marylander and close personal aide who was frequently included in command secrets, to bring the news to Philadelphia. Tilghman, although recovering from a fever, raced out of Yorktown in a small boat but soon ran aground. Forced to spend the night on the islet where he grounded, he made little progress the next day because of a poor wind. Thirty miles below Annapolis, the wind failed completely and Tilghman again became ill. But he got ashore, found a horse and streaked off toward the Capital. After changing horses several times, he entered Philadelphia, cold, miserable and unsteady, at midnight on October 23. According to Lossing, he aroused Thomas McKean, President of the Congress, who in his unrestrained joy ordered the Great Bell rung until dawn broke over the city.

According to the Minutes of the Assembly, this is what happened:

October 24, 1781. The Bell was rung "by order of the Council" at 12 O'clock noon this day to announce to the people the surrender of Cornwallis to the Confederate arms of the United States and France — a day of the most intense interest, joy and rejoicing of the people. The standard of the State was hoisted to the peak of the belfry over the State House. Four pieces of artillery responded to the pealing of the Bell and all the city bells answered.

The time of the ringing seems unimportant. It is enough to know that the Bell contributed its part to the joy that swept through the city on that brisk October day in 1781.

But the joy that spread through the city was not entered into by all, and the city fathers apparently expected some disturbances. A broadside was hurriedly printed and copies of it posted in prominent places. It read:

ILLUMINATION

Colonel Tilghman, Aid de Camp to his Excellency General Washington, having brought official accounts of the SURRENDER of Lord Cornwallis, and the Garrisons of York and Gloucester, those Citizens who chuse to ILLUMINATE on the Glorious Occasion, will do it this evening at Six, and extinguish their lights at Nine o'clock.

Decorum and harmony are earnestly recommended to every Citizen, and a general discountenance to the least appearance of riot.

The last paragraph was doubtless directed at those who might be considering Quaker-baiting; the Friends did not go along with the custom of illumination in connection with war. But the crowd was in festive humor and the Quakers were fair game. Elizabeth Drinker relates the events of the evening in this way:

Ye 17th of this month, October [1781], Gen'l Cornwallis was taken, for which we grievously suffered on the 24th, by way of rejoicing. A mob assembled about 7 o'clock or before, and continued their insults until near 10, to those whose houses were not illuminated. Scarcely one Friend's house escaped. We had nearly 70 panes of glass broken; ye sash lights and two panels of the front Parlor broke in pieces . . . ye Door cracked and violently burst open, when they threw stones into ye house for some time but did not enter . . . Some houses, after breaking ye Door, they entered and destroyed the Furniture, etc. Many women and children were frightened into fits and 'tis a mercy no lives were lost.

But the overexuberant mob eventually quieted down and the city returned to a more normal existence than it had seen during the

ABOVE: the State House in 1778 with its steeple intact. OPPOSITE: the building as it appeared in 1799 with the steeple removed and the Bell lowered to the louvred section of the tower. *National Park Service.*

active war years. While the war was considered over, minor skirmishes and clashes occurred from time to time until gradually, peace enveloped the land.

For the most part, the Bell was rung joyfully in the years that followed, beginning with Washington's triumphant return to Philadelphia on November 27, 1781. It rang to herald the signing of the Peace Treaty with Britain in 1783 and harmoniously announced the adoption of the Constitution four years later. It rang when the Federal Capital was established in New York in 1789 and presumably — although it is not recorded — to signal the removal of the Capital to Philadelphia in 1790. It rang in the admission of new states and the inauguration of Presidents, and mournfully tolled the news of Washington's death in 1799.

That same year the Commonwealth of Pennsylvania moved its state capital to Lancaster, and in 1812 to its present location in Harrisburg. Then, in 1800, the federal government moved from its temporary home in Philadelphia to the newly-completed city of Washington, District of Columbia — a seat that would remove it from the boundaries, and influence, of any one state. Having no better use for the State House, the legislators leased Charles Wilson Peale the building's second floor and Assembly Room for his natural history museum. Exhibits of all sorts were installed, and visitors paid twenty-five cents for admission.

Thus at the turn of the century, the Great Bell ceased to serve the Pennsylvania Assembly, although it continued to be rung for important occasions. However, in 1816 the Bell was to face a near disaster, one of two it would endure in a twelve-year period. The Pennsylvania Legislature, needing funds for a new Capitol Building at Harrisburg, decided to sell the State House and the grounds it stood upon. The original scheme was to appoint a group of commissioners who would divide the land into building lots and sell them at public auction. It was thought that the property should bring not less than $150,000. The State House, standing proud and regal, would presumably be sold for whatever the materials within it would bring, and the scrap items would, of course, include the Great Bell. The only objects that were thought worth taking to Harrisburg were the clockworks and its two faces. Fortunately for the Bell and the State House and our entire American heritage, an alternate plan was offered in which the city of Philadelphia would be permitted, if it so desired, to purchase the building for $70,000. All Americans can be

thankful that the city acted on the proposal and acquired the State House and its grounds. The Bell was saved.

But 1828 was to bring another brush with disaster and the seemingly magic life the Bell possessed surfaced in time to save it once more. In that year Peale's museum was removed and the City of Philadelphia decided to renovate the State House. William Strictland designed a new steeple in a style similar to that of the original, but larger and with provisions for a new, four-faced clock, and one John Wilbank was contracted to cast a new bell "Twice the size of the Great Bell" to be used in conjunction with this clock. The contract stipulated that Wilbank was to receive the Great Bell, appraised at $400.00, as scrap. After sizing up the situation, Wilbank balked, stating that drayage costs would amount to more than the Bell's worth. So saying, he refused to move it, leaving it hanging where it was. Angered, the city fathers sued him for breach of contract and Wilbank, anxious to avoid legal troubles, paid court costs and presented the Great Bell to the City of Philadelphia as a "gift." Today Philadelphia still owns the Bell, although by contract it is under the custody of the National Park Service.

Wilbank provided a new bell for the clock and the Old One remained on its lower level of the tower beneath the new steeple. The louvres were replaced by glass windows that could open, and the Great Bell continued to be rung, joyfully or sorrowfully as the events demanded, for state occasions. Having rung wildly in 1824 to welcome the Marquis de Lafayette back to Philadelphia and honor France's role in the American Revolution, it dolefully sounded again in 1834 to announce his death.

Then, on the 8th of July, 1835, it was given the sorrowful task of tolling the death of Chief Justice of the United States John Marshall as his remains were made ready for the journey to Richmond, Virginia, where he was to be buried. The tradition handed down to us holds that on that day the Bell cracked and its tolling for Marshall was its last. While it may have cracked, this was not its last peal. Records show that it was muffled and tolled at the death of President William Henry Harrison in 1841 and, finally, it was declared permanently out of commission when, after repairs had been attempted, it was rung for Washington's Birthday in 1846.

The
Last
Clear Note

INVESTIGATIONS BY METALLURGISTS IN RECENT YEARS HAVE shown that the Great Bell suffered from an inherent illness that may have begun with the crack made when it was first hung in America. It was melted down and recast twice after that and additional metal added to it, and such treatment tends to weaken metal. Thus the weakness did not stem from the many moves it made while awaiting repairs to the tower. Perhaps the biggest shock it received was the one sustained in Bethlehem when its wagon collapsed. How severe a shock that was cannot be determined but it was, nonetheless, one that could only serve to further sap its strength. The beginnings of the crack that rent the Bell when Marshall's body was carried from the city in 1835 may have been present in a formative state for many years. When the Bell was rung for Washington's Birthday in 1846, it was literally the Bell's final blow with its clapper.

Ironically, the Great Bell had not been slated for ringing on that particular birthday. It rang as a reflection of the frustration of the city's Municipal Legislature and a somewhat obstinate stand taken by a church. As the birthday approached, the lower chamber, called the Common Council, adopted a resolution authorizing the ringing of church bells to celebrate the anniversary. It was implicit that two churches would be so designated — St. Peter's and Christ Church. The reason was simple; they were the only churches possessing full eight-bell rings at that time.

However, the Municipal Legislature was bicameral, and the directive from the Common Council necessarily had to come before the upper chamber or Select Council, which amended the resolution to specify only Christ Church as the bell sounder for the great occasion. In unusual language, it further specified that Christ Church was claimant to the exclusive ringing of the bells because Washington attended that church when in Philadelphia and stated that the church "will not do so unless it attains the whole sum usually given by the city for this service to the illustrious dead. The sum is thirty dollars."

Obviously, members of the Select Council had contacted Christ Church and learned that that body would be happy to ring their bells if the entire fee would be directed only to itself and not split with St. Peter's. The situation surely precipitated some lively debate and neither of the two councils yielded. St. Peter's, meantime, declared that it would be happy to accept half the fee in order to gain the honor of ringing for our first President's birthday. The arguments mounted and apparently continued for days. News of this difference of opinion inevitably reached the press and, on publication of the story, solutions to the delicate problem were forthcoming from a number of quarters. Finally, in somewhat embarrassed desperation, the Common and Select Councils, briefly uniting in opinion, acted on a suggestion that the State House Bell be employed in ringing the honors. And so the Legislature got off the hook by announcing that ". . . the old Bell in the State House should be struck through the day." This left Christ Church out in the cold and caused great disappointment at St. Peter's, which had been willing to compromise.

More important than the solving of a dispute between the two churches, however, is the fact that the decision to make strenuous use of the aged Bell was tantamount to the signature of its death warrant. On February 26 the Philadelphia *Public Ledger* reported the details of that unhappy February 23rd:

The old Independence Bell rang its last clear note on Monday last in honor of the birthday of Washington and now hangs in the great city steeple irreparably cracked and dumb. It had been cracked before but was set in order for that day by having the edges of the fractures filed so as not to vibrate against each other, as there was a prospect that the church bells would not chime upon that occasion. It gave out clear notes and loud, and appeared to be in excellent condition until noon, when it received a sort of compound fracture in a zig-zag direction through one of its sides which put it completely out of tune and left it a mere wreck of what it was. . . . It has been suggested that it should be re-cast; and as it is now entirely useless, but composed of good stuff, the suggestion is entitled to consideration. It can never be replaced but by itself, and although it may not be improved, yet, pure as it is, it can be re-formed to much advantage. [This last, of course, facetious.]

And that is how the Bell came to be silenced, although not forever. It was still to give forth sound, but only by the stroke of a special rubber hammer.

The big question, of course, is: what happened to the Bell that left it "irreparably cracked and dumb?" What made it crack? Speculation on — and possible answers to — the question were not forthcoming until 1915 and 1916. On May 24, 1915, a letter appeared in the *Public Ledger*, signed by Alexander E. Outerbridge, Jr., a metallurgist at The Franklin Institute. He completed a profound study of the Bell and its crack and then made this pronouncement:

Recent scientific investigations have shown that when metal, similar to that of which the Liberty Bell is composed, is re-melted several times under careful supervision, it loses 'resilience,' or banding quality, becoming brittle like glass. . . . It is no hyperbolical figure of speech to say that the venerated Liberty Bell is afflicted with a serious disease. Metallurgists have adopted into their technical jargon the term 'diseases of metals,' and recognize several with maladies. I have no hesitation in saying that the bell has . . . distemper.

It was entirely possible, according to Outerbridge, that several factors contributed to the Bell's malaise. The brittleness of the first Bell might have started the whole thing, in spite of Whitechapel's denial that it was too brittle. Pass and Stow did not help the situation to any degree when they added copper to the Bell's mixture for strengthening purposes, and, when *their* first Bell clonked instead of clanged, they may have added more tin in an attempt to bring back the tone. In summing up, Outerbridge stated:

> Under the circumstances, the casing cannot possibly have been of a homogeneous composition, and the bell was, therefore, subject to abnormal shrinkage and cooling strains.

A year later, writing in *Numismatical and Antiquarian Society Proceedings,* Wilfred Jordan acknowledged the deleterious cooling strains and clarified the situation even further:

> The Liberty Bell is suffering from an organic disease of long standing. As with many people, a disorder might be called hereditary and date from birth. So the defects of this old relic date from the first casting in England. This organic trouble arises from the scientific truth that all metal castings are subject to internal strains due to natural shrinkage in cooling. These are known as 'cooling strains' and the . . . fracture in the Liberty Bell was most probably due to such a cause. . . . Each time the heavy clapper struck the bell, the molecules contiguous to the flaw were thrown into violent vibration and what is known to metallurgists as 'breaking down in detail' took place. . . . In plain words, the crack extended at first perhaps only a millionth of an inch. . . . Such a minute flow may . . . [have taken] years to reach the surface, even under the vibrations caused by the strokes of a bell clapper. . . .

Satisfactory or not, these are the only seemingly logical explanations for the crack in the Bell. A new crack was detected in 1907, an extension of the original, and it appears to extend above the crown. This leads to an intriguing question: could the new crack eventually ascend to the top of the crown and start down the other side of the Bell? And would that ultimately lead to splitting the Bell in half? Probably not. The Bell today is solidly braced inside and treated with the greatest of care and respect.

A close-up of the famous crack showing the file marks left by William Eckel and the second crack starting at the "P" which opened during the Bell's journey to San Francisco in 1915. At the time this photograph was taken, the bolts had been removed for inspection of the Bell. *National Park Service.*

It is interesting to note that when the damaged Bell was designated to ring for that fateful Washington's Birthday, William Eckel, Superintendent of the State House, tried to repair it using almost the same technique that Edmund Woolley had apparently tried ninety-four years earlier on the first cracked Whitechapel Bell. Eckel filed and drilled the crack, making it wider to lessen the vibrations which might easily cause even further damage. When he had finished this work, he swept up the filings and had a small bell cast from them. He then presented this to the Committee on Public Property in Philadelphia which in turn gave it to the Pennsylvania Historical Society. Unfortunately, its disposition today is unknown.

Inevitably, a flaw as celebrated as the crack in the Bell must give rise to legend. The legend of the crack begins, of course, with John Marshall but, oddly enough, variations on the legend did not begin to appear until 1900. The files of the Independence Hall National Historical Park contain a transcript of a letter to the Philadelphia *Public Ledger,* undated. It carries the following information:

To the Editor of the *Public Ledger:*

Sir — in June, 1903, Charles W. Alexander wrote the Public Ledger as follows concerning the Liberty Bell: "The bell was not cracked tolling for the death of Chief Justice Marshall in 1835." Quoting from Wesley Bradshaw's History of the Old Liberty Bell, and corroborated by the official record in the Journal of City Council for 1828: "It was cracked during the violently joyful ringing at LaFayette's visit to Philadelphia in 1824, but not completely disabled until one night in the following winter, when, while ringing an alarm of fire, it finally gave out."

A seemingly logical story, and one that can not be entirely discounted. But an article in the *New York Times* for July 16, 1911, transcends all legend by relating an eye-witness account of the cracking of the Bell — by a man who claims to have helped crack it in his youth. The story was imparted in an exclusive interview with eighty-six-year-old Emmanuel J. Rauch of Philadelphia. He told the *Times* reporter an astonishing story of the events leading up to the cracking of the Bell on Washington's Birthday in 1835. He was about ten years old at the time. This is how the *Times* wrote it, quoting Mr. Rauch:

. . . On that day [Washington's Birthday] I had been sent by my mother on an errand to a shop not far from our house. On my return from it, I was walking through State House Square when I noticed that the janitor or steeplekeeper of the old State House building was beckoning to me. His name was Downing — "Major Jack" we used to call him — and he was a well-known character in Philadelphia at that time.

"Come here!" he called to me and to several boys whom he spied in the square. After he had corralled six or eight of us — I don't remember exactly how many — he told us that he wanted us to ring the Liberty Bell in honor of Washington's birthday. The idea pleased us very much — we boys were not in the habit of ringing the old Bell — and we agreed to do it.

Then Downing climbed into the steeple of the State House and tied a rope to the clapper of the Bell. Coming down again, he put the end of this rope into our hands and instructed us to pull with all our might, which we did.

We were working away and the Bell had struck, so far as I can recall, about ten or a dozen times, when we noticed a change in the tone. We kept on ringing, though, but after a while the steeplekeeper noticed the difference, too. Surmising that something might be wrong, he told us to stop pulling the rope. Then he climbed back into the steeple, we boys following behind.

On the side of the Bell that hung toward Walnut Street, we found that there was a big crack, a foot or fifteen inches long. Downing then told us to run along home. We obeyed.

What happened after that I forget; boy-like, I didn't do any worrying and heard no more about the cracking of the Bell until some years later. Then, however, and many times since, I have read of how the Bell came to be cracked, but never have I seen the version which I have just given. I honestly believe it to be the correct one.

It is not beyond possibility that the crack did in fact become noticeable at that time, five months prior to tolling the death of John Marshall.

Other versions of the fatal fracture have appeared from time to time. One dates it to when the Bell was rung in honor of a visit of Henry Clay to Philadelphia; another as the result of a ringing to announce the British Parliament's passage of the Catholic Emancipation Act in 1828. Historians today, however, are in almost unanimous agreement that the Bell was seriously damaged when rung for John Marshall in 1835 and that subsequent use compounded the injury. William Eckel's attempts to mend the crack only served to freeze it in place — but in so doing, he gave permanence to an aspect of the Bell that the late Miss Victoria F. Smith of Philadelphia described in her delightful talks at Independence Hall National Historical Park. "The crack," she said, "symbolizes the imperfections inherent in a democracy."

The first use of the State House Bell in a publication. It appears over a poem "suggested by the inscription on the Philadelphia Liberty Bell" published in an 1839 abolitionist pamphlet. *National Park Service.*

Birth and Rise
of a
Symbol

T HE MID-YEARS OF THE NINETEENTH CENTURY WERE PERHAPS the most important of all periods in the Bell's history for they were to mark both its death as a serviceable bell and its birth as a national symbol. Until these years, the Bell had received little or no attention beyond the confines of Philadelphia. When it was proven irreparable in February of 1846, it once more came close to destruction by being, in the words of the *Public Ledger,* "composed of good stuff" and worthy of recasting. But again, perhaps because of its sheer weight, no one made the effort to remove it from the tower. As of November 27, 1848, Benson J. Lossing, in his *Pictorial Field-Book of the American Revolution* records the Bell as still hanging "in silent splendor." It was not until the hundredth anniversary of the Bell's arrival in America that it awoke to its new role. In July, 1852, it was, in the words of Thompson Westcott, "removed from its framework in the tower and placed upon a temporary pedestal in Independence Hall, when the convention of delegates from the Thirteen Original States was held for the purpose of concerting measures for the erection of a monument in Independence Square to commemorate the Declaration of Independence." The Old One had emerged from its chrysalis and would soon become the celebrated Liberty Bell.

Both of the writers quoted above had accepted in good faith a totally fabricated story about the Bell written by George Lippard, a nineteenth-century author who was not above drawing on his imagination when the facts were lacking. And so they reproduced Lippard's story with their own modifications. There is no basis whatever for the "blue-eyed-boy-and-old-man" myth.

Ironically, the first recorded use of the term "Liberty Bell" comes not from Philadelphia but from Boston, and the "Liberty" for which it stood was neither religious nor political, but Black liberation from slavery. In 1839 an early Boston abolitionist group calling itself "Friends of Freedom" circulated a pamphlet which presented as its frontispiece an idealized rendering of a bell encircled by the familiar inscription and captioned "Liberty Bell." The bell is shown suspended from the branch of a tree and the ground beneath is strewn with broken shackles. Inside the pamphlet is a "sonnet" inspired by the Bell, which reads:

> It is no tocsin of affright we sound,
>   Summoning nations to the conflict dire; —
>   No fearful peal from cities wrapped in fire
> Echoes, at our behest, the land around: —
> Yet would we rouse our country's utmost bound.

Six years later a similar abolitionist pamphlet appeared in Boston, this time with a poem by Bernard Barton in which he proclaimed:

> Liberty's Bell hath sounded its bold peal
> Where Man holds Man in Slavery! At the sound —
> Ye who are faithful 'mid the faithless found,
> Answer its summons with unfaltering zeal.

In 1847 a longer poem with the title "The Liberty Bell" by R. R. Marden was included in another of the abolitionist booklets which had begun to foretell the Civil War. One verse read:

> Oh for a glorious peal at last
> Of the true bell of Liberty!
> To rend the air, and strike aghast
> The monster might of Slavery.

The first published true likeness of the Bell over the caption "Liberty Bell" appeared in Lossing's *Field-Book* quoted above, and in his text Lossing wrote: "Here upon this dusty beam, leaning against the old 'Liberty Bell,' let us sit awhile and peruse that brilliant page in our history. . . ." Lossing's book, which contained observations recorded in 1848, was published in thirty parts between 1850 and 1852, and later in two volumes. In it he gives a brief history of the Bell, ending with the now-famous legend of the "blue-eyed boy, clapping his hands and shouting 'Ring! Ring'" to the "gray-bearded" old man in the tower of the State House upon the announcement of the Declaration of Independence. Joel Tyler Headly, another popular historian of Lossing's time, picked up the thread and in 1854 published the legend as a part of his serialized "Life of George Washington" in *Graham's Magazine,* followed shortly after by a book of the same title.

In Lippard, Lossing and Headly "The Old One" found its publicity agents and gained fame under the name "Liberty Bell." As with much of the popular historical writing of the time, their books were crammed with anecdotes, legends and descriptions, a blend of facts and fancies that only an expert could separate years later. But the American public was unconcerned with factual accuracy; the fancies and legends made better reading and added lively color to the new-found symbol. The Liberty Bell embodied the essence of American freedom and ideals in a tangible relic that, unlike the Declaration itself, could safely be touched and seen and reproduced in symbolic illustrations and three-dimensional replicas.

Following its removal from the tower in 1852, the Bell began its to quarters within the State House, which by now was generally called Independence Hall. It was first placed on display in the Assembly Room, where it stayed for twenty-six years. Next, it was moved to the hallway of the building and, shortly thereafter, moved to the Supreme Court Chamber. In a dramatic move, it was next

GRAHAM'S MAGAZINE.

VOL. XLIV.   PHILADELPHIA, JUNE, 1854.   No. 6.

The Bellman Informed of the passage of the Declaration of Independence.   (See page 562.)

The cover of Graham's Magazine, June 1854, gave the Bell national recognition and led to the myth of the "blue-eyed boy." *National Park Service*.

suspended from the ceiling of the Tower Room by a thirteen-link chain. It was later returned to the Assembly Room, set in a glass case, and then hauled back to the Tower Room. Its glass enclosure was removed, leaving the Bell open for all to see and touch.

In 1885, a new chapter in the life of the Bell began, one which took it on a series of random journeys across the United States and into New England and the Deep South. It was to cover more than twenty-five thousand miles in these highly controversial excursions and be seen by millions of Americans who might otherwise never have become aware of its existence and growing symbolic status.

Its first departure from Philadelphia came about as the result of an invitation from city officials in New Orleans, who urged that the Liberty Bell be sent to that city for display at the 1885 World Industrial and Cotton Exposition. Patriotism and strengthening of ties between North and South were put forth as arguments for dispatching the Bell to Louisiana. The Mayor of Philadelphia and other high officials thought well of the idea and on January 23, elaborate preparations were put into motion to send the Bell south. The pomp, circumstance and carnival atmosphere which surrounded the Bell on its journey to New Orleans offered an astonishing contrast to the first journey of the Bell — the furtive exit from Philadelphia in a farmer's wagon.

The Bell's trip to New Orleans was remarkable in the magnitude of ritual, ceremony and general pretentiousness which accompanied it nearly every minute of the way. A description of that specific journey serves well as a composite of those that would follow.

When the decision to send the Liberty Bell was made, the first step was its unhanging. Taken down from its pedestal in the Tower Room, the aging relic (it was now 132 years old) was given a scrubbing and polishing that caused it to shine brightly and probably destroyed the patina it had carefully gathered through the years. Once clean, it was placed on a specially built platform truck just outside Independence Hall where it is said to have attracted a great deal of attention.

The following morning, the truck was covered lavishly with bunting, flags and evergreen arches. Nestled within its leafy bower, the Bell now became the focal point of a procession wending its way out Market Street to the West Philadelphia Station. Newspaper accounts

By 1856 when this Max Rosenthal print was made, the Bell had been saved from oblivion and was displayed in the Assembly Room of Independence Hall. The eagle perched on the Bell was from Peale's Museum and is still preserved at Independence Hall National Historical Park. *National Park Service.*

of the day relate that a forty-eight-man Honor Guard marched beside the truck as it was drawn to the terminal by six "gayly-caparisoned horses." Following the truck and its guard came cornet bands, mounted Reserves, two military battalions and the committees who arranged the trip (all city officials). Crowds lined the street as the procession moved westward, cheering the Bell on its way.

Once at the station, the Bell was transferred to a flat car which had been dressed up with a decorative wooden railing. On the car was positioned a wooden yoke from which the Bell was suspended. The phrase "1776-Proclaim Liberty" was lettered on the yoke and the car itself bore the words "Philadelphia-New Orleans" emblazoned on streamers strung along its sides. Centered between the names of the two cities was a drawing of clasped hands.

That preparations had been made hurriedly is evident in the fact that workmen were still battering at the Bell's fastening bolts as the train steamed slowly out of the station. But now the Bell was en route and the ovations accorded it along the way were more than gratifying to those who had arranged the journey. People pressed to see the Bell, to touch it, to kiss it wherever it stopped and, in Virginia, the ultimate tribute was paid to it by Jefferson Davis, head of the Confederacy during the Civil War. According to historian Charles F. Warwick in *The Keystone Commonwealth,* Davis struggled from his sick bed to see the Bell. Davis pondered it and then said: "I believe the time has come when reason should be substituted for passion and when we should be able to do justice to each other. Glorious old Bell, the son of a revolutionary soldier bows in reverence before you."

On reaching its destination, the Bell was greeted by surging crowds who displayed, as described by Victor Rosewater, "rejoicing unequalled in the city's record of festivities." The Bell's appearance in New Orleans was a smashing success and the return trip to Philadelphia was accompanied by as much ritual as had marked the journey

The Bell on one of its travels passing through Plainfield, Connecticut, in June 1903, on its way to Boston. *National Park Service.*

south. Mayor Guillotte of New Orleans, together with a party of city officials, rode with the Bell as far as Baltimore where, in great ceremony, the venerable relic was turned over to the safekeeping of Philadelphia's Mayor Smith, who had gone to Baltimore with his own party of city officials. With much pomp, the Bell was received by its original guardians and escorted back to the Quaker City.

Its arrival in Philadelphia was marked by the firing of guns, a parade of numerous organizations escorting it back to Independence Hall and a riotous display of flags and bunting festooning homes and businesses along the way. The entourage paused at Mayor Smith's house where a huge floral replica of the Bell with the word "Welcome" wrought in flowers, wreaths and a proliferation of flowers and flags awaited its arrival. Along the route the Bell was virtually smothered with floral pieces and evergreen arches and, so garlanded, reached Independence Hall late in the afternoon of June 17 after an absence of nearly five months.

To top off the occasion, Mayor Smith gave a banquet that night to celebrate the Bell's return and to honor the visiting Mayor of New Orleans and his court of city officials and policemen. The festivities were enjoyed by all and the only dark note cast upon the entire venture was put forth by the comptroller of the city of Philadelphia. When he received bills in the amount of $1,397.82 for the costs of the banquet, he refused to pay them, stating with much determination that it was highly illegal to spend public money for "entertainment, eating, drinking and smoking." How the bills were resolved is not known.

The success of the New Orleans trip encouraged the promoters of the Columbian Exposition in Chicago to request a visit from the Bell and so, in 1893, it journeyed west to the Windy City. The same festive atmosphere attended it all the way and again its appearance was enormously successful. President Cleveland made a short address to honor the Bell as it passed his hotel on the way to the exposition; the return from the Fairgrounds was a bit more somber. Chicago's Mayor Harrison had been assassinated shortly before.

Routed back to Philadelphia via Allentown, the Bell was placed in a trolley car and hauled up the hill to the church where it had been hidden during the Revolution. A night pageant was arranged and the festivities continued into the next day, when the Bell left for home. One estimate of the number of people who had viewed the Bell during the trip to Chicago and back placed the figure at twenty million.

A scant two years later, the Bell was invited to attend the Cotton States and Atlantic Exposition in Atlanta, Georgia, but now trouble loomed. A group of concerned citizens in Philadelphia, fearing for the safety of the Bell, attempted to obtain a court order preventing it from leaving the city. The action was defeated and the Bell traveled south once again, arriving in Atlanta on October 3, 1895.

Returning in February, 1896, the Bell enjoyed its comfortable berth in Independence Hall until January 6, 1902, when it again headed south, this time to Charleston, South Carolina, to be displayed at the Interstate and West Indian Exposition. June of 1903 found the Bell in Boston, paying a quick, five-day visit to that city in honor of the Bunker Hill Celebration.

In 1903, the Bell went to the Louisiana Purchase Exposition in St. Louis, Missouri, for just over five months. After St. Louis, the Bell rested until 1908 when it was taken briefly from Independence Hall and paraded through the streets of Philadelphia to mark the city's Founders' Week celebration. Participants in the parade, which was an historical pageant, were all dressed in period costume with the exception of the three drivers of the flat truck bearing the Bell. They were dressed in contemporary clothes and all wore derby hats.

The next departure, in 1915, followed the Bell's participation in a most historic occasion. On February 11, direct telephone communication between the east and west coasts had been officially completed and on that day the Bell was gently tapped in Philadelphia and its sound sped across the continent over the telephone wires, thus becoming the first "live" sound to be transmitted from coast to coast. The sound was received in San Francisco by Mayor Rolph and other dignitaries who then engaged Mayor Blankenburg of Philadelphia in conversation. At one point Alexander Graham Bell, who was listening on a third instrument in Washington, D.C., cut in and reminisced about his own visit to Philadelphia's Centennial Exposition in 1876, when he had first publicly demonstrated his telephone.

After the conventional ceremonial dialogue between the parties in Philadelphia and San Francisco, Mayor Rolph put in a strong bid to

Cesar Chavez, left, and George Meany hold a grape box beside a White-chapel bell wrapped in chains to symbolize the plight of California grape pickers on strike in 1970. The chains were removed in July of that year after the dispute was settled. *Wide World Photos.*

display the Bell at the forthcoming Panama-Pacific Exposition, soon to open in the Golden Gate City. When news of this invitation reached Philadelphia's citizens, another storm of protest arose, but San Francisco was determined to have the Bell. A fiercely aggressive campaign was now instituted by that city in its effort to bring the Bell west. Two hundred thousand California school children signed a petition asking for the Bell, a resolution in the state's legislature echoed the request and numbers of prominent Californians sent messages requesting that the Liberty Bell be displayed at the Exposition. President Wilson became involved in the fracas, endorsed the move (although there is some doubt about his interest in the matter) and the Californians won when Philadelphia's City Council voted its approval.

Now the protest against the Bell's removal rose to epic proportions. The Council's action was blasted from all sides and words like "outrage," "betrayal of trust" and "offense against . . . community and . . . country" were hurled about with alarming frequency. Charges and accusations were made and the arguments voiced most loudly were three.

First, it was said that a "milk and water" type of patriotism motivated the carting of the Bell about the country, the purpose seemingly being to encourage a spirit of national loyalty. Second, crass commercialism was noted. The appearance of the Bell at fairs and expositions could only serve to attract greater numbers of people and bring more money to the promoters. Third (and this hurt the city fathers most), it was bluntly stated that the journeys of the Bell were "an unblushing effort" on the part of city officials to go visiting and sightseeing around the nation at public expense.

The charges and accusations, however, did not block the trip, but city officials, mindful that the protesters feared for the safety of the Bell, had it carefully examined to be sure it could make the western trek without damage. Out of this came the construction of a special "spider," a device to shore the Bell and distribute its weight more evenly. The ancient relic made the trip to San Francisco and back without incident and thereafter left Independence Hall only twice more, each time briefly and within the confines of Philadelphia.

On October 25, 1917, the Bell helped spur the first Liberty Loan drive in Philadelphia by parading through the streets in a public display of patriotism. Its last venture from the sheltered Hall of Independence occurred in May, 1919, when it was moved out and in front of the Hall to salute the return of Pennsylvania's famed 28th (Keystone) Division from World War I.

Replicas and
Reproductions

BECAUSE OUR LIBERTY BELL IS IN ITS OWN DISTINCTIVE WAY A superlative bell, it is only natural that descriptives applied to it quite logically fall into the superlative. It is the most famous bell in the world (and that simple statement describes it best) and it is the most legend-ridden (and therefore the most misrepresented). It is the most widely-traveled bell in the world and the bell most seen and touched and venerated by the people of the country it symbolizes. There are other "mosts" that can be used in describing it, but perhaps the most astonishing is found in the knowledge that it is the most duplicated, imitated and scale-reproduced bell on the planet.

Beginning in 1753 with the small bells cast by Pass and Stow from Whitechapel's original, the list of reproductions made to scale or to size, or simply by calling another bell a "Liberty Bell," is almost endless. When William Eckel, superintendent of the State House steeple, widened the crack in the Bell in 1846 to permit its sound to be heard on Washington's Birthday, he made the small facsimile noted earlier from the drillings.

114

In the years that followed, no record of "official" duplication of the Bell exists, but one will never know how many hundreds of thousands of souvenir bells were made and sold to an eager public. Each exhibition of the Bell on its many travels spurred new souvenir-making in addition to the countless little replicas sold both at Independence Hall and in gift shops across the nation. Some of the small reproductions were functional. During the 1920s, for example, banks purchased Liberty Bell penny banks to give new customers. Decorative table models and mantle objects were made in great numbers, as well as paper weights for businessmen's desks.

In two-dimensional form, the Bell has appeared on countless medals, plaques and carvings of various kinds and its likeness has been imprinted on stamps and coins and in untold millions of photographs, official and amateur. The sesqui-centennial year — 1926 — found it on a commemorative stamp. The recent Ben Franklin half dollar features the Bell on its reverse side. Many prints (not all of them depicting the Bell in accurate scale) have been made available to an eager public and paintings delineating momentous occasions in the life of the Bell have been preserved.

Replicas, both full size and to scale, turn up in many unexpected places. Some are "replicas" in name only but are, nonetheless, called "Liberty Bells" to honor the original. The "Liberty Bell of the West," for example, was cast in France in 1741, ten years before the Whitechapel Bell was cast, shipped to this continent and hauled more than eight hundred miles overland to the Catholic Church of Kaskaskia, then a town on an island in the Mississippi River. Although weighing only 650 pounds, just under one-third the size of the Great Bell in Philadelphia, this bell added its lusty pealing to that of many around the land when news of the adoption of the Declaration reached the distant outpost. It is still, to the people of the Midwest, a personal symbol of America's struggle for liberty.

In 1876, Mr. Henry Seybert, a prominent Philadelphian, decided to donate a new clock and bell for use in Independence Hall tower. It was given in commemoration of the hundredth anniversary of Independence. Cast by Meneely & Kimberly, Founders, of Troy, New York, the bell weighed thirteen thousand pounds, each one thousand pounds representing one of the original thirteen Colonies. A verse from St. Luke appears on the crown. "Glory to God in the highest and on earth peace, good will toward men." Encircling the brim is Norris' original quotation from Leviticus: "Proclaim Liberty throughout all the land, unto all the inhabitants thereof." On the bell's waist is seen the inscription: "Presented to the City of Philadelphia, July 4, 1876, for the belfry of Independence Hall, by a citizen."

The bell was placed in the steeple and rung to celebrate the Centennial, but it had to be unhung and sent back to Troy for recasting in September of 1876. Returned in November of that year, it has hung in the tower ever since and serves as a clock bell. The bell it replaced — the 1828 Wilbank bell — was sent to Germantown's Town Hall, where it hangs today.

The "Columbian Liberty Bell" was cast in 1893 and used to promote interest in the Chicago World's Fair, where the original Bell was displayed for several months. The "Women's Suffrage Liberty Bell" was sent around the country as propaganda for the suffrage movement. After it had done its work and the Nineteenth Amendment

The Bell as used on the Franklin half-dollar and the Sesquicentennial commemorative stamp. *Photos by Ken Young.*

Several bells from a series of 2400 small "Bicentennial" replicas being cast at Whitechapel are lined up in the same moulding room where the original State House Bell was cast in 1752. A gold plated bell from this series was presented to President Nixon in April, 1973. *Courtesy Liberty Bell Limited Editions.*

gave women the vote, the bell was presented to the Washington Memorial Chapel at Valley Forge.

In 1926, on the occasion of the Sesqui-Centennial of the nation's independence, a group of six "Liberty Bells" was brought from the exposition and placed briefly around the Great Bell. These bells, so called because they had rung when the Declaration was made public, came from Easton, Reading, York, Lancaster, Chester and Allentown, all cities in Pennsylvania. A bell was donated to Louvain University in Belgium in 1928 by the American Society of Civil Engineers and other American engineering societies to commemorate American members of their profession who had given their lives in World War I. It is inscribed, and known as, the "Liberty Bell of Louvain." Other "Liberty" bells in foreign locations can be seen today in Hrad Castle, Prague, in Tokyo and in Tel Aviv, and there are probably still more.

The federal government, in 1950, undertook a large-scale mass reproduction of the Bell to assist an intensive drive to sell Savings

Bonds. Fifty-three bells were cast at a foundry in Annecy, France, each an exact duplicate of the Liberty Bell in size, tone and inscription, but with the crack etched in outline on the surface. A bell was given to each of the then forty-eight states, Alaska, Hawaii and Puerto Rico. One was presented to President Harry S. Truman and is now in the Truman Library at Independence, Missouri, and the last was given to the District of Columbia, where it now can be seen at the west entrance to the Treasury Building.

Materials for the bells were gifts of the brass and bronze industries in the United States and the steel industry furnished metal for their mountings. A motor company provided forty-nine trucks to take them to each state and to Washington, D.C. Location of the bells was left to the governors of the recipient states and most are now placed on or near capital grounds. The Pennsylvania bell, as noted earlier, was presented to the Liberty Bell Shrine at Allentown, where the Great Bell went into hiding in 1777.

One of the 53 replicas cast at Whitechapel in 1950. This is the Pennsylvania bell, now in the Liberty Bell Shrine in Zion's Church, Allentown, where the Liberty Bell was hidden during the winter of 1777-1778. *Photo by John Hinshaw.*

Ringing
for
Freedom

THE LIBERTY BELL TODAY STANDS QUIETLY IN ITS WISHBONE-shaped cradle atop the pedestal where it has rested since 1915, just inside the south doors of Independence Hall. The pedestal is actually a movable dolly which can be sped through the doors and into the square behind the hall in the event of an emergency such as fire. Thousands of people visit it daily and its accessibility to touch is more than gratifying to those who journey to pay it homage.

The Old Bell, older than independence itself, has enjoyed an enormously colorful life, despite its disability. It has narrowly escaped destruction several times, most recently in 1965 when members of a radical movement were arrested and charged with planning to blow it up along with the Statue of Liberty and the Washington Monument. It has witnessed seven major wars involving our country and watched its growth from a mob of upstart rebels in '76 to a leading world power. The Bell almost went into hiding for a second time during World War II when an insurance company offered to build a bomb shelter for it. The offer was accepted but later dropped because of difficulties in obtaining necessary priority materials.

The Bell came close to being repaired on two occasions, a circumstance which most certainly would have diminished its image in the eyes of its country and the world. On the first occasion, in 1876, a committee was appointed to consult with one Joseph Ruhback for purposes of putting the Bell in condition to be rung on the Centennial Fourth of July. A forceful protest against such a move apparently went up immediately; a resolution later presented to the Council by the committee indicated that "the people prefer that the Old Bell shall remain in its present condition." The second brush with restoration came when Mr. Albert A. Hughes, one of the two proprietors of Whitechapel Foundry in England offered to recast the Bell as a symbol of friendship between America and Britain. His offer, made in 1945 at the close of World War II, was graciously declined.

In 1950, the City of Philadelphia turned over the administration of Independence Hall and its surrounding property to the U.S. Department of the Interior, National Park Service. Since then, an extensive program to restore the hall and the areas adjacent to it has been under way. A beautiful mall now stretches north from Independence Hall, made possible by the razing of buildings considered dilapidated and historically worthless which faced the hall for many years. Early houses and public buildings in the neighborhood of the national shrine are undergoing similar restoration and the eventual effect will be of an area somewhat like it was in the eighteenth century, if one can ignore the twentieth-century embellishments of electricity and automobiles.

Today the Bell is the focal point of a drive toward a more logical method of celebrating the Fourth of July, namely the ringing of bells across the nation at two P.M. Eastern time on the Fourth so that the entire nation, with one simultaneous sound, would commemorate the adoption of the Declaration of Independence. This movement was begun by author Eric Sloane in 1962. He was joined in his effort by another writer, Eric Hatch, who is now devoting as much time as possible to furthering the ringing of the bells. Sloane modestly disclaims total originality for the idea, noting that bell-ringing served to honor the Fourth for about one hundred years but somehow fell into disfavor after the Civil War, undoubtedly because of the increasing use of fireworks on the occasion. He also notes that John Adams, in the letter to his wife following the adoption of the Lee resolution stated that he thought the ringing of bells should mark the anniversary of the Second of July in future. The Sons of the American Revolution had also experimented with the idea in North Carolina in 1961 and the following year attempted to make it a national custom. Only a few chapters of the Society responded, but the movement was under way.

Then, in 1963, Connecticut's Senator Abraham Ribicoff brought up the subject in the Senate and gained a resolution, with the House concurring, that "bells should be rung on the holiday and that civic and other community leaders should take appropriate steps to encourage public participation in such observance." Ribicoff's proposal and the resultant resolution were published in the Congressional Record for February 28, 1963, under the headline, "Let Freedom Really Ring."

Next, President John F. Kennedy issued a proclamation declaring that "Bells mark significant events in men's lives. Birth and death, war and peace are tolled. Bells summon the community to take note of things which affect the life and destiny of its people. The Liberty Bell rang to tell the world of the birth of a new country's freedom. Next Thursday, the Fourth of July [1963] when the bells ring again, think back on those who lived and died to make our country free. And then resolve with courage and determination to keep it free and make it greater."

With such powerful support, the movement has been gaining momentum, gradually but forcefully. It was not until 1972, however, that the Liberty Bell itself was recruited to help the cause. On July Fourth of that year, the Pennsylvania Society of Sons of the Revolution launched "Operation Patriotism." In order to give it strength, the Bell which had remained mute through most of the years since the San Francisco telephonic transmission, was pressed into service. It had been tapped, but not rung, in the intervening years, most notably on New Year's Eve, 1925, when it was sounded to herald the dawn of the 150th Anniversary of Independence, and on June 6, 1944 — D-Day — when it was heard in a solemn sounding beseeching safety for the men who were about to invade Western Europe.

Now, however, it would be utilized as the springboard for the ringing of bells everywhere to commemorate the reading of the Declaration. The ceremony was confined to chapters of the Revolutionary Sons, but previous publicity had made their intention known nationally. And so, on July 4, 1972, at exactly two P.M., Mrs. Dorothy Charlton Hauck, Assistant-Secretary General of the Society of Descendants of Signers of the Declaration of Independence and herself a descendant of signer John Hart, New Jersey's delegate, stood in front of the Bell and signaled for thirteen strikes on the Bell in the Tower of Independence Hall, once for each of the thirteen Colonies. These stirring sounds were transmitted over telephone lines to Mount Morris, Illinois, where the state's Governor Richard B. Ogilvie was presiding over a concurrent ceremony. While somewhat localized, the ritual of the Bell served to demonstrate the appropriateness of bell ringing on the national anniversary.

It's not unlikely that the ringing of bells will be the dominant sound on future "Fourths," and it is intriguing to reflect upon the idea that our Liberty Bell, a symbol of freedom everywhere and now voiceless, perhaps forever, will itself become symbolized — by the ringing of other bells.

Selected Bibliography

Adams, John. *Letters to His Wife.* 1876.

Drinker, Elizabeth. *Extracts from the Journal of (1759-1807).* New York: Lippincott, 1889.

Ditzel, Paul. "The Story of the Liberty Bell Since 1751," *American Legion Magazine,* December, 1968.

Dow, George Francis. *The Arts & Crafts in New England, 1704 1775.* Topsfield, Mass.: The Wayside Press, 1927.

Etting, Frank M. *The Old State House.* Philadelphia: Porter & Coates, 1891.

Faris, John T. *The Romance of Old Philadelphia.* Philadelphia: Lippincott, 1918.

Franklin, Benjamin. *The Papers of Benjamin Franklin.* Edited by Leonard W. Labaree & Whitfield J. Bell, Jr. Vols. 4 & 5, July 1, 1750 to March 31, 1755. New Haven: Yale University Press, 1961 & 1962.

Gabriel, Ralph Henry, Ed. *Pageant of America.* New Haven: Yale University Press, 1927.

Hawke, David. *The Colonial Experience.* Indianapolis: The Bobbs Merrill Co., Inc., 1966.

Independence Hall National Historical Park. Research files. Philadelphia.

Ingram, Tom. *Bells in England*. London: Frederick Muller, Ltd., 1954.

Jordan, Wilfred. "The Liberty Bell," *Numismatical & Antiquarian Society Proceedings,* Vol. XXXVII.

Kaufmann, Henry J. *American Copper and Brass*. Camden, N.J.: Thomas Nelson & Sons, 1968.

Lippard, George. *Legends of the American Revolution*. 1847.

Lossing, Benson J. *Pictorial Field-Book of the American Revolution*. Philadelphia: George W. Childs, 1852.

Malone, Dumas. *The Story of the Declaration of Independence*. New York: Oxford University Press, 1954.

Pennsylvania Gazette, The. 1749-1754, all issues. Philadelphia.

Pennsylvania Journal & Weekly Advertiser, The. 1748-1754, all issues. Philadelphia.

Person, Morgan D. *The Liberty Bell Shrine*.

Marshall, Christopher. *Diary of Christopher Marshall*. 1839.

Norris, Isaac. *The Isaac Norris Letterbooks* and the *Fairhill Letter Collection*. Manuscripts, The Pennsylvania Historical Society.

Riley, Edward M. *History of the Independence Hall Group Transactions of The American Philosophical Society*, Vol. 43, Part 1, 1953.

Rosewater, Victor. *The Liberty Bell: Its History and Significance*. New York: Appleton, 1926.

Scharf, Thomas J. and Westcott, Thompson W. *History of Philadelphia 1609-1884*, 3 vols. Philadelphia: L. Everts & Co., 1884.

Stoudt, Rev. John Baer. *The Liberty Bells of Pennsylvania*. Philadelphia: William J. Campbell, 1930.

Van Doren, Carl. *Benjamin Franklin*. New York: The Viking Press, 1938.

Votes and Proceedings of the House of Representatives of the Province of Pennsylvania 1744-1758. Philadelphia: 1774.

Watson, John F. *Annals of Philadelphia*, 2 vols. Philadelphia: 1884.

Index